Whose Lit

Dr. Kisha Roberts-Tabb

Whose Little Girl Am I

©2018

ISBN-13: 978-1726312097

ISBN-10: 1726312097

Dedication

I dedicate this book to my heavenly Father for creating me for such a time as this.

I dedicate this book to all the ancestors who fought and died so that we may live. To my entire ancestry from mother Africa whom created a sense of pride that we were able to bring with us across the Atlantic Ocean.

I dedicate this book to all of my female ancestors who walked the stairs of Elmina and Cape Coast Castle being taken at every level. To all the ancestors that exited the door of no return and headed to new lands.

I dedicate this book to all my ancestors who landed on plantations and worked cotton fields, breast fed master's kids and worked the big house. All who fought and revolted against the conditions of slavery. Those who forced the hands that led to the emancipation.

Dr. Kisha Roberts Tabb

I dedicate this book to my entire lineage that worked so that we may live better lives. To my great grandparents Roy and Anna Roberts who established traditions that carried us through every obstacle.

I dedicate this book to my grandparents Warren and Cynthia Roberts along with Paul and Bernice Chandler for giving us everything they had, for being THE best grandparents in the world. Life on 35th established us not as only cousins, but it gave me the best friends I ever had, and for that I dedicate this book to you all. My grandparents modeled a work ethic that ensured we would become productive members of our families, community and society as a whole. My grandmothers taught me how to be a God-fearing woman. They taught me scripture and how to pray. These women taught me how to walk in grace and appreciate His mercy.

I dedicate this book to my entire family all my Aunts and Uncles for insolating me with so much love that the outside world could never penetrate.

I dedicate this book to every client that I was able to impact, understanding that I was able gain so much more from them, than I was ever able to give.

I dedicate this book to my squad, the bomb beauties that I call my friends I love you ladies.

I dedicate this to my bonus babies Arion, Kentaris, Kentrae, Shirkyra, and K.J. My bonus moms Marilyn and Donna. My sister/cousins Qiana, Tanara and my Brother/Cousin Anthony.

I dedicated this book to my siblings Kimyona, Brandi, Briana, Kristin, Omari and Kalene. Your love, support and loyalty have carried me over every bump I ever encountered.

I dedicate this book to my parents Warren and Tanya Roberts whose love produced the queen who stands before you. My mother, whose public struggle became my private strength. My mother's ability to live life on her own terms has bestowed a confidence in me that has taken me further than I ever imagined. My daddy, the man that gave up his life to raise his kids. The man that showed me what real love looked and felt like. The man who put a crown on my head and adjusted it every time I lost my way.

I dedicate this book to my baby girl Jaylah Mae, my something to live for, my everything. My new beginning and my second chance. Your smile, confidence and beautiful essence has inspired me beyond greatness. Being your mother has been the greatest experience of my life.

I dedicate this book to my King, best friend, foundation, and husband, Chuck. You have been my biggest supporter. You have allowed me to explore the depths of my desire and ability. Picking me up each time I fell and encouraging me to try again.

Dr. Kisha Roberts Tabb

Acknowledgment

There are so many things in life that will make you forget how blessed you are. I have been blessed with an amazing village. A village that have supported me through all my endeavors.

Thank you to Ariana Misher, Dr. Kimyona Roberts, Briana Roberts and Jaylah Roberts-Coleman for contributing to this project.

Thank you to Jonathan Willis for assisting in setting the sound track to this project.

Thank you to Sheridan S. Davis and Chocolate Chip and Co. for everything that you have done to make sure this project was successful.

Music has set the soundtrack for my life, I thank every artist that is quoted in this book for making such amazing music and sharing your gift with the world. Thank you for lyrics and

Dr. Kisha Roberts Tabb

rhythm that has allowed me to dance through life.

Whose Little Girl Am I?

Dr. Kisha Roberts Tabb

TABLE OF CONTENT

Dr. Kisha Roberts Tabb

INTRODUCTION

"Don't you ever JUST feel like a lil girl from the projects?"

I answered, "Yes all the time!"

Honestly, that question didn't sit well with me; so, I pondered over it—not so much the question, but my answer. I was cool with being a girl from the projects. In fact, I was quite proud of my IDA B. WELLS roots. It was the "JUST" that didn't sit well with me.

The more I thought about it I have said this a million times: "I'm 'JUST' a girl from the projects!" "I'm 'JUST' a little Black girl from the Hood!" When I felt a little more empowered, I'd say "I'm enough 'JUST' the way I am!" When I was dealing with a break up or rejection, I'd say, "I'm JUST right, something must be wrong with them." But the truth is my life's journey was full of determination and persistence, not "JUST" anything.

I've tried to live my life by Jeremiah 29:11, which reads,

" For I know the plans I have for you declared the Lord plans to prosper you and not to harm you, plans to give you hope and a future."

I love the way it is written in the Message Bible. It says,

"I know what I am doing. I have it all planned out plans to take care of you, not abandoned you, and plans to give you the future you hoped for."

If I truly believed and lived a Jeremiah 29:11 life, the JUST did not belong in my vocabulary, and honestly, it never did.

My Journey began with loving teen parents who married and later divorced. My education began at my neighborhood school. After the first day, my mom decided I didn't belong there and I was transferred to a neighboring school outside my district. It was a perfect fit. My parents volunteered, my sister, cousin, and I were involved in everything. I even wrote a play for the DARE graduation in 5th grade. A top standardized scorer, I missed four questions on the bench mark test. Only four, that is great, right? My father insisted that the score sheet be pulled, and discovered that I missed the last four questions. In his eyes, I had giving up and that was just unacceptable.

It was around that same time that my secret began to surface. The kids at school started to notice the decline in my mother's appearance and began to talk. Now to be fair, I'm not sure if the kids were that mean or if I was consumed by my own thoughts. Either way, I had to get as far away as I could from anyone who knew her or that she was my mom. So, I persisted and convinced my dad to transfer me to a school in Hyde Park.

I felt like an alien there. I thought all the kids there were rich—I was JUST a lil girl from the projects after all. The first semester there I received my first D. Actually, I received my first five D's. I will never forget report card day was the same day James Brown had been arrested, and like him, I was confined for five months - a month for each D. No television, radio, telephone, or going outside. All I could do was read. I had gotten a D in spelling so my dad made me write out the dictionary. I made it all the way to the letter M before the news confirmed that Mandela was being released from prison. Honoring his impact, my dad ended my punishment early. From that point, on I was persistent in my studies and I graduated from Louis Wirth Middle School as Valedictorian.

High school was mediocre at best; I had more fun than anything. Now, in high school I was convincing my teachers to allow me to make up work and do extra credit. Because of my grades, I spent a lot of time on punishment reading. So much so that I later realized I had read every book on my freshmen reading list for college. I do not believe this was just a coincidence, nor was the decision to return home after my first year of college, but we will get there.

My mother's addiction had taken her places neither I nor she could imagine; she emerged with HIV/AIDS. Knowing that we would need to understand her new life moreover, her impeding death, she convinced my sister and I to join support groups and peer training. After losing her battle, I volunteered and fought to bring awareness around the issues of women and girls with HIV/AIDS.

Two years after losing mine, I became a mother. This prompted me to finish what I had started three years earlier and return to ISU. Not only was my Financial Aid denied but the University no longer accepted my previous classes. Again, I persisted and fought to have both decisions overturned. I won! Three years later I graduated with a scholarship to study abroad at the University of Ghana Legon, a scholarship that had first been awarded to another student who couldn't accept due to child care issues. So, in essence I received a scholarship that I never applied for. Just another one of those "coincidences."

Upon returning from Africa, I was determined to be impactful first by teaching and then working at Juvenile Court. Upon arriving, I began to recognize my ability to relate to my female clients. I began to see my passion and the possibilities of this passion in the eyes of my girl clients. Years later, four other women and I founded SOCIAL Butterfly Foundation Rites of Passage and Mentoring program. Over a five year span we were able to impact over 80 girls. This was definitely no coincidence, SBF taught me to honor those who God had chosen to walk beside you.

With the fundraising success of SBF, I was approached to assist in fundraising for the

Dream Center's Farm for Human Trafficking Victims. Instead, I decided to donate all of the money that was needed as long as they agreed to dedicate the space to my mother, Mrs. Tanya Lynn Roberts. Avoiding many requests to come visit the farm I did agree to an outreach ride along.

That night it was confirmed I did not just have a passion for working with girls and women, it was my life's purpose to assist women and girls who had been afflicted by addiction, low self-esteem, abandonment, exploitation, violence, or just because she was born female.

That night lead to the creation of my current position, the completion of my dissertation, a Ph.D. in Community Psychology, the development of the Resilience Trafficking Triage, and Roberts-Tabb & Associates.

Was this all just a coincidence or was it all part of the plan to prosper me and not be harmed?

Dr. Kisha Roberts Tabb

1 COFFEE

"The clothes she wears, her sexy ways make an old man wish for younger days…"

-The Commodores, 1977

My momma was always a pretty woman. Caramel complexion, slanted eyes, and a small frame. Needless to say, she was fine. I always wanted to look just like her, but instead I looked just like my dad. I was high yellow and longed for her sun kissed glow on her perfectly tanned brown skin. Although I was told that I was shapely, still I yearned for her small petite figure. There was something about the way she stood that made her look like a real-life silhouette. Her face was perfectly chiseled with defined cheek bones that highlighted her deep set, slanted brown eyes. Momma was my version of a super model.

Not the models of old but the exotic ones that we see now. If you didn't know her, you would think she was Somalian. She didn't have what we call "good hair," but she styled it in soft finger waves. Momma was way before her time. This very hair style is being worn by so many millennials. She dressed like something out of a magazine, her style was incredible and always out of the box. I mean who can pull off a polka dot blouse with a butterfly collar and a tied waist belt? The queen of a jumpsuit and a wide brimmed hat, my momma was fly.

No matter how many complements I received, I knew that I looked nothing like my momma so I could not possibly be pretty. I would find myself standing back on my legs to give the impression that I was slightly bow legged like she was. Although she didn't have the type of butt that would make you stare, her tiny waist made her look like she had a perfect coke bottle figure. She was beautiful; I only wish she thought so. Instead she focused on the spots on her face, believed that she was too skinny, never appreciating the uniqueness of her face, the brightness of her smile. I would have giving anything to look like her. In fact, I would purposely spend extra time in the sun, trying to get her caramel colored skin tone. As you can imagine in the summer time, when my tan was right, you could not tell me anything. I practiced my smile in the mirror trying to get that perfect curve that caused her cheek bones to sit extra high. I even learned how to do my own finger waves. I bet if you asked her she would have told you that I hated everything about her, when in actuality I hated everything about me that was contrary to her. I felt the prettiest when I looked like her.

I wish that she could have seen herself though my eyes. She would have seen this dope chick that made clothes look good and not look good in clothes. Through the lenses I saw her through she was so smart and so sweet. I wish she could have loved herself half as much as I loved her. I wish that she had looked to me for validation and not the men in her life. I promise I would have done anything to put her on cloud nine; she didn't need drugs for that. I wish she could see us now. Combined we are a perfect reflection of who she was. Just like my momma, we are FLY!

2 A LONG RIDE

"You said you would never leave in the summer…"

–Common & Lauryn Hill, 2004

I've been on this bus for 8 hours and I have 6 hours to go. I have taken this ride to Pine Bluff a million times but this time it seems extra-long. I can't believe that I'm actually on the way to one place and Pee-Wee is somewhere else. Since I was 13 years old, my entire life has been about him. I almost lost him to that stroke and I never left his side. I stopped going to school, I stopped hanging with my friends, I rarely went home to my own family. To be honest, before the stroke when I was with my family, so was he.

I come from a huge family, seven brothers and one sister. I am number eight and my baby brother is my heart. Tanya and Jo-Jo were inseparable even in our relationships, he even went with Pee-Wee's lil sister. I'm definitely going to miss my little brother. I've heard tell of people going to Africa and getting off the plane feeling like they have arrived home. That's how I felt when I got off the Greyhound in Pine Bluff. The air even felt different down here. Although I'm going to miss Pee-Wee, I think this is a great move. Hopefully he will visit me here and fall in love with this place the way I have.

Just as I settled in to my life as a country girl, I realized that my period had not come and to be honest I can't remember when the last time I had one. My aunt Mable had made several comments about the glow of my skin and the spread in my hips. I decided to get a test, I took the test and a large, bold, pink plus sign appeared. What was I going to do? This is supposed to be my new beginning. I am only 17. How am I going to tell Pee-Wee that I am 600 miles away and pregnant with his child?

3 COLOR HIM FATHER

"Now little ol' browned eyed girl..."

Gil Scott-Herron, 1974

They say that a girl's first love is her daddy. In my mind the sun rose and shined because my daddy woke up. In my mind he was the best thing since sliced bread. I can remember standing outside each day waiting on him to get off the #4 Cottage Grove bus. As soon as he turned the corner around Supreme Life, my sister and I would take off running. It was one of the best parts of the day. The problem is when you place a person so high on a pedestal the fall is so hard. Don't get me wrong, I still think that he has something to do with the sun rising, I now realize that he is a human being and not a super hero, and yes, he is capable of making mistakes. I also know that sometimes our expectations of people don't always line up with their ability. When I think back on the unrealistic expectations that I had for my dad to be perfect it almost seems unfair.

A divorced man, living in a bachelor pad with his brother in law, living the *single, single, life*, and then here I come. A 9-year-old girl imposing on their pad. When I first arrived at my dad's house, I thought I had died and gone to heaven. Pizza every night, his lady friends doing my hair, buying me clothes, buttering me up in order to stay in his good graces. It was great. Then the rules came. I want you to picture the scene in *Boys in the Hood* when the dad, Furious, started telling his son Trae all of the rules and the chores, Trae responding "so what you gone do?" That's exactly how this played out, with the exception of the "what you gone do?" I was way too afraid of my dad to say anything close to that, at least not to his face.

Life with Pee-Wee was no joke; you better not go to bed without washing the dishes. Good grades were a must, he didn't except anything less than a C, and even these were disappointing. I can remember begging teachers for extra credit to ensure that I did not get a C. I can clearly remember his face when he learned that I had missed four questions on my fourth-grade standardized test. The disappointment I felt, because he believed that I just gave up. Now that I think about it, I wonder if it was true. It was definitely true so many times after that. I often wonder if my dad's shared opinion of me that day in Mrs. Hudson's classroom was a self-fulfilling prophecy that shaped how I tackled life thereafter.

Believe it or not, my daddy's opinion of me shaped every decision I made. From what type of car to buy to my college major. The question of what would my daddy think always remained in my head. His opinion of me was so important that when I decided to date the neighborhood drug dealer, I kept it from my daddy. I went so far as to making him use an alias when he called the house.   For two years I was dating Matthew as far as my Dad was concerned. Living in a high-rise building made it easier to get in and out of his car without my daddy seeing me. He was raising me to be an African Queen and here I was auditioning to be the neighborhood B-girl.

No matter how hard I tried, I seemed to always disappoint my daddy. I wonder at times if his friends were aware of all the mess I had put him through. I can recall over hearing him say "I don't worry about her I know she will be ok." However, what I processed was *I don't care what she does*. This was devastating. Had he washed his hands of me? How could he not worry about me? If he knew all the mess I had been involved in he would see he needed to worry about me. What was I looking for? The truth is he didn't know me because I had become two different people Daddy's Lil Girl in front of him, and someone that I barely recognized in the street. What father in his right mind would allow his daughter to come and go as she pleased while she chased behind a man, who at any moment could have been the target of gang retaliation? The expectations that he set seemed so unobtainable. I struggled with rather or not I deserved the title or throne of a queen.   I now know that my Daddy saw something in me that was greater than anything that I could have imagined. I wish that I could see what he saw when I looked in the mirror. I was only able to see my short comings while he saw my potential.

"Your Daddy Loves You, Your Daddy Love His Girl…" - *Gill Scott Herron, 1974*

Dr. Kisha Roberts Tabb

4 THE SPLIT

"Cause we made it this far on for better or worse..."

-Tamar Braxton, 2013

P
eople in the projects thought we were the black version of the Cleavers. We looked like the perfect family. A stay at home mother, two daughters, and a father that worked two jobs. Everyone loved to come to our house, a lot of times they would come and never leave. My parents were some sharp dressers and could throw a party like no other. They looked good together, but when the doors closed and everything went back to normal they fought like cats and dogs.

"We'll be chillin' and laughin' and laying on your chest. Don't know what happened cause things just went left." -Tamar Braxton, 2013

34

They would go from being the most loving couple to throwing bowls of cereal at each other in an instant. It was always hard to process how you could love someone so much and act like you hated them all at the same time. One of my fondest memories of my parents is my mother taking lunch to my dad downtown and the four of us outside eating the lunch that my mother had prepared for her family. The two of them made grocery shopping fun and putting the groceries up in our yellow painted kitchen exciting. As young as I was, I can still remember the look of love in the eyes of my parents.

My saddest memory was the two returning home without the daughter that had been born. This was the first time I had seen my dad cry. I also recall the look of rage in my father's eyes as well as that of fear in my mother's. Did he blame her, did she blame herself?

Even as a young child I knew that my mother's loyalty and need to fit in with her friends would cost our family. I can remember the look of frustration when he would return home from work and Momma was in the room with a group of her friends, leaving my sister and I in the living room in front of the television. That look on Daddy's face meant it would be a long night for us.

More often than not we began to go to Sunday dinner on 45th without Momma. In fact, it became so frequent that no one even asked where she was anymore. We would arrive home to find her with that glossed over look in her eyes.

Honestly, I don't remember when my Daddy officially moved out I just, know that at some point around second grade he didn't come to 536 with us anymore. I knew that he had begun to work more and even later, now he would still come to her parents' house on 35th Street, but I couldn't recall the last time he shared that apartment with my mother. Eventually it became apparent that I no longer belonged to a two-parent household. One night after Sunday dinner, my dad and grand-dad dropped us off. One look at my mother's glossed over eyes and I began to protest this new living arrangement. After all, no one asked my sister and I how we felt about our new home environment. Hell, they didn't even sit us down and talk to us about the split the way they did on TV. I was not having it I placed myself between Momma and Daddy holding the door open attempting to stop my dad from leaving. In hindsight I'm not sure if I was trying to make him stay or if I wanted to go with him. In the midst of the struggle, I ended up on the outside of the apartment with my dad. My mother slammed the door shut catching my baby finger in the heavy metal door. I began to scream and my dad began banging on the door. Fearing my dad was trying to get in the house to fight my mother, she would not answer, my finger was severed. I lost that battle but the war between my parents continued.

5 THE NEW ME

> "I woke up this morning looking back over the dark of my life. Things for me is not what they use to be."
>
> *-Areatha Franklin, 1976*

I never really felt pretty. I mean I never had a problem getting a man, I just didn't understand what they saw in me. But I was always glad they saw something because I sure as hell didn't. Believe it or not, I was good at faking it. I even faked my way through my wedding. Don't get me wrong, he was my first love, my first boyfriend, he was my FIRST. I wanted to be his wife but for the life of me I couldn't figure out why he wanted me to. On the day of the wedding, I stood in front of the mirror desperately wanting to feel pretty. I had on an ivory dress, the bustier adorned in beads. Momma couldn't stop talking about how beautiful I was. As pretty as the dress was I felt like a hot mess in it.

All my friends told me I had a great life. I had a husband whom I loved and loved me, but I had no idea what love was until I saw my children look up at me. I also never knew what lost was like until I lost one of my children. Even with all that I had, I never felt worthy of any of it. I faked it though! When we were out I was the life of the party, hell it wasn't a party until I got there. Everybody knew that I was down. Not my marriage or motherhood could keep me from a party. I started every party with a joint and a drink. I tried some of everything but nothing really did it for me. Nothing took away the image of my lifeless baby girl in my arms; so, I stuck with my joint and my drink.

I was at a party at my girl's house she told me she couldn't wait for me to try this bass. Bass? What the hell did I want with a damn guitar at a party? Chile let me tell you it sho' wasn't no

41

damn guitar. The first time I hit that pipe and I heard that bell ring in my head I was in love. Suddenly I felt prettier and more worthy of all the attention that I was getting. After every hit I felt sexier, less inhibited, when I looked in the mirror I could see what all those guys saw. This erased the image of my baby girl. I would smoke and smoke and smoke, for days on end. My husband was complaining about all the company in the house— he didn't understand these were my friends. All he did was work and when he wasn't working he was out playing, at least that's what I had convinced myself. The truth of the matter was we didn't have anything in common anymore. He still smoked weed but he wouldn't touch that pipe, he made me swear that I wouldn't either—and I wouldn't—as long as he was around. Before I knew it, all I did was hit that pipe. I don't know how the kids got to school; I don't know when my husband left; hell, I don't know when they took the kids. All I remember is that I had some high highs and some even lower lows and a bunch of men in between. Every time I saw my kids I had a new man.

After eight years of none stop smoking and screwing, I'd had enough. I was ready to get clean, get my kids and husband back, get my life back. So, I went to treatment and did well too, for about 3 months. I got out to the same friends, same neighborhood, but no husband and no kids. What the hell was I staying clean for anyway? After three rounds of treatment and relapsing, I finally got it right, I needed to stay clean for my kids I had missed most of their lives already. I was ready for a different life and I got it. I stayed clean, got my GED, my kids came over every weekend. We were really getting it together. I couldn't believe how much they had grown up, they were young ladies now. I enjoyed listening to their weekly events and what boy they were liking. I loved being able to give them their mother back, I wanted to make sure that I remained responsible. I set up a savings account one for each one, I even went to get me some life insurance. Ain't that a trip? Before getting clean, all I knew was right now. Now here I am thinking about what if. I was loving my life, my kids, my job, and my new place. From the outside, it may have seemed boring but for me my new life was exciting I was on a ride and was going to stay on it just to see how far it would take me. I'd recently signed up for some classes, so when I saw the white envelope with no return address, I assumed it was my first set of grades, nothing could have prepared me for what was in that envelope. I had been denied life insurance and needed to come in and speak to a doctor. This was a damn insurance company, not a hospital. But I am responsible now so I made the appointment. I arrived sat down in the doctor's office and was absolutely devastated by what he told me. How could this be? I never shot up. I was just getting

my life together. How was I gone tell my kids?

They'd just gotten their mother back. My kids.

6 THE VIOLATION

-John Legend, 2008

I t was the Sunday before Martin Luther King's birthday and the fight to make it a national holiday was all over the news. Momma decided that we would go to Ann's house. I was not sure if she was a family member or a friend. I did know that I couldn't remember a time when I didn't know her or her kids. She had to be family because her sister Pat was my Auntie, wasn't she? Either way, we always had fun when we were all together. She had two boys and a girl although they were much older than me and my sister, it was always fun to be around them. Like most of the times when the adults were together, the kids were confined to a room either the front room or a bedroom depending on where the adults decided to be. This time the grownups were in the kitchen which meant we had to go to the boys' bedroom because her daughter wasn't home. After entertaining each other -while the boys did who knows what, I went to ask my mother something just to find that she had "made a run". I was ordered back to the room until she returned, and I obeyed. When I got back to the room, the boys asked if I wanted to play a game. Excited that the big kids wanted to play with us, I said yea. He asked me to lay on the first bunk and he was going to put a pillow over my head and I had to guess what they were doing. I said ok. I laid down, the pillow went over my head. I assumed my sister was either reading or waiting for her turn to play the guessing game because I didn't hear her say anything. The older brother began to whisper directions to the younger brother. I couldn't make out exactly what was being said. I did make out the tug on my pants. I immediately became afraid, actually paralyzed. I began to squirm and then I felt the pressure on the pillow get harder. I felt my pants being pulled down but my panties were still on. I remembered Momma's warning about anyone going into my panties touching my private parts. My panties were my protection. "Maybe they are going to hide my pants and I have to guess where they put them," I thought. They were both always nice to us even treated us like their little sisters. "They wouldn't do anything to hurt us, would they?" Then I felt someone hold my ankles down and even in my second-grade mind I knew that we were no longer playing a guessing game. I knew that whatever came next was not going to be fun or right. I felt a hand on my forbidden panties but it wasn't the yank that I expected I felt a hand moving my panties, then air. I became paralyzed, unable to move. Where was my sister? It was only two of them, if one had my legs and the other was holding the pillow over my head while moving my panties over, they couldn't be doing the same thing to her. Maybe if I just lay here and let them do what they want they won't bother her. Are they making her watch this? For the first time in my life, I hoped that she is reading. I laid there and tried to think of anything but what was happening, I tried to think of something that would allow me to deal with the pain that I was expecting. My thoughts were interrupted by the feeling of something wet. What was this? It didn't hurt, it felt weird and nasty all at the same time. I had no idea what was going on but I wanted it to stop. I began to squirm and the grip on my legs became tighter. If I had to guess I would say this was the first time I prayed. I mean really prayed, "God please let this stop." Trying to stay as still as I could, afraid that if I move the grip on the pillow would get tighter. Desperately wanting this to be over, I lie there until I no longer felt the wet sensation and the grip on my ankles loosened. I still didn't hear my sister but I did feel someone get off the bed then the pressure from the pillow subsided and I could hear a second set of footsteps exit the room. All I could do was get dressed, I grab my sister and pray again that my Momma was back. She wasn't. I decided that my sister and I would stay in plain sight until my mother returned. But when would that be?

Dr. Kisha Roberts Tabb

7 536

"Cloud nine you can be who you want to be cloud nine you ain't got no responsibility…"

-The Temptations, 1969

The smell that consumed our small project apartment was one that I will never forget. I could identify this smell anywhere. The musty smelling smoke didn't smell like the Kool cigarettes that my mother smoked. It also smelled different than reefer, which was a familiar scent. This was new and it smelled horrible. The funny thing is that I only smelled it when the door of my mother's room was closed and other people were there. As I watched "She Ra" on the television in our empty living room, my mother would emerge from her room with a mirror that she held high and close as if she was trying to keep something from wasting. The clinking of glass and metal filled the kitchen while she boiled something. I assumed it was dinner until she finished and headed back to the room only emerging to do this ritual again. That night dinner never happened. Each time she emerged from her room her eyes looked larger than before. They were eyes that didn't even seem to notice that my sister and I were even there. Days like this became a normal occurrence in our household. It amazed me how many people were able to fit into her small bedroom. As the weeks turned into months, our apartment, which had been nice based on project standards, became grim and bare. Every week items disappeared, the radio, our bikes, the Atari, our Sesame Street record player, the telephone, and the TV. Before long, the house contained nothing more than a let-out couch, a kitchen table and an empty refrigerator. The days of full cupboards after Momma had gotten her check, had long gone.

In fact, there were many days when we arrived home to an empty house and had to climb through the back window to get in. It wasn't long before I could pick up the glazed, over bucked look in her eyes to know that she had been in her bedroom, or at least someone else's. The change in my mother's behavior allowed a certain amount of freedom that we were not previously afforded. We were able to stay outside as long as we wanted, she never cared if we stayed over to friends' house, and often left us with her friends who had children. Wanting to ignore the change in the quality of our lives, my sister and I never discussed her among ourselves or to others. We quickly learned that Momma's presence was a little more than a guest from day to day. Needing to eat more than a daily school lunch and an occasional school breakfast, we began to spend every evening after school at my grandparents' house. On 35th I knew we would get a good meal, the chance to watch TV and interact with someone other than each other. When we were home alone I did most of the talking. Kim spent most of her time reading and ignoring me. Grandma's house was headquarters and I was sure that if my mom had come home and we weren't there, the first place she would look was 3545. One of my mother's mini-vacations lasted longer than normal. We contemplated calling Daddy but decided against it. At this point, they hated each other and if he knew what had been going on he would kill her. Instead, we walked to the pay phone and called Grandma. Before we knew it Grandma, who had never visited our project apartment, was there with my auntie and that was officially our last day as Ida B. girls. My mother didn't protest our abrupt removal from her care, and she never attempted to get us back. There were no indignant arguments of "How dare you take my kids without telling me!"

She didn't burst infuriated into our grandparents' house and demand that we get our things together to go home. We were just there. I often wondered how long it took her to return home and notice that we were even gone. Whose little girls were we now? The truth is, it changed with the seasons.

Dr. Kisha Roberts Tabb

8 NO RETURN

"Sometimes I feel like I am all alone..."

-John Legend, 2008

My momma was what you would call a free spirit. She did it all her way, including being a mother and wife. The favorite auntie, cousin, and friend, everyone loved to come to our house. My momma's house was like a never-ending slumber party— all were welcomed! She would make popcorn balls, her famous Tanya Taco's and Grape Kool Aide with just the right amount of lemon. Our house was lively, full of spirit, decorated so vibrantly. Bright yellows and baby blues colored the walls. I always said that my mother was before her time. Before her time. That would explain why she always seemed to be looking for something, she was trying to contain herself in a time and space that was not ready for her to occupy. To the outside world she seemed to have it all but eventually, she would walk away from it all.

I can't tell you when the sun stopped shining in our window, but I do remember that day by day our lively apartment turned into a fortress. What seemed so vibrant became so dim. More often than, not we used the window to gain entry because no one was there to let us in. My mother's presence became more sporadic, leaving us for days on end. When momma finally realized that we were gone and not coming back, she also took refuge at my grandparents' home. Although we had been reunited under my grandmother's roof it did not mean that we were able to return to our mother-daughter covenant. My sister and mother seemed to pick up right where they left off, but for me, a wall had been built. The in and out, the ups and downs had become too much for me.

I wanted my momma back but where was she, the woman that made appearances at my grandma's house was nothing like the woman that helped me with my homework or did it for me when it got too late. Where was the woman that would rub my head when I got a headache? Where was the mother that was so attentive to her children, dressing them up like twin porcelain dolls on holidays? Where had she gone and would she ever return?

Walking home one day, I saw my mother and a man at the corner of 37th and King Drive. I yelled her name to get her attention. They were walking so fast you would've thought they were exercising. Seeing that it was me, she crossed the street leaving her male acquaintance waiting impatiently. Although I acted like I didn't care that she was never around the truth is I missed my momma and I wanted her back. Not knowing when our paths would cross again, I took this opportunity to ask my momma to come home. This was her opportunity to choose me. "Ma, come to grandma's house with me. Kim is there." I figured throwing Kim in there would give me a little leverage. I began to tell my momma all of the things that had been going on with us, all the things that she had missed. She stood there trying to listen but the shake in her leg let me know that our time together was coming to an end. The guy across the street was visibly becoming more and more impatient; so I began to beg. "Momma please come with me," my begging quickly turned into sobbing and the man across the street began to call her name. Torn between my tears and his request to "let's go", my mother turned back and forth between the two. He won. She turned around and crossed the street to join her male counterpart and began walking away. I screamed "Ma... Ma...Momma!" I stood on that corner screaming and crying until she had faded completely out of my sight.

I would never beg another person to do anything as long as I lived. That day, I realized that we had reached a crossroad in our mother-daughter relationship. That day we had reached the point of no return. I had reached the point of no return. For as long as I can remember, I have proudly stated that "I don't ask nobody for nothin'." I would rather suffer than to feel that type of rejection. I would NEVER return to that pitiful little girl begging to be chosen, to be loved, to be valued. Well, at least not until I met a boy.

Dr. Kisha Roberts Tabb

9 FIRST DAY OF SCHOOL

"You say the right thing to keep me moving on to keep me going strong..."

-Brandy, 1995

I don't know how I did it but I had managed to convince my father to let me transfer to a new school. Here, I could hide, I can keep my secret. No one here would ever know that my mother was addicted to crack. Here, I was safe. My Aunt lived a block from the school and her closet became my mall. The day before school started, I had already picked out every outfit I would wear that week. A Fila Jogging Suit, Donna Karen top, and a few other labels that I knew no one from my old school had ever heard of; but this was Hyde Park.

I arrived at the school a half hour early. I stood anonymously amongst the crowd waiting for the bell to ring. I had chosen this school because it started in 6th grade so everyone would be starting over. To my surprise, they had all went to the elementary school together two blocks away. I didn't care that I didn't know anyone, in fact, I LOVED IT. I didn't know them and they didn't know me, my mother or my secret. It was perfect! Everyone at my old school called me Keisha, even though my name was actually **Kisha.** Here, I could be Kisha and that's exactly how I introduced myself, well the new me.

Then in the midst of the playground rush to get in line, a girl approached me and said, "Hey what's your name?" As proud as I could I said, "KISHA." It sounded funny coming out of my mouth. I had stopped correcting people in 2nd grade, but I was so glad that I could actually be the girl that I was born as. Not the girl the neighborhood or my classmates had made me. Interrupting my thoughts this girl asked me,

"Who's in recovery? Is it your Mom?" Damn, I just can't get away. How did she know? Mistaking my feeling of being exposed for confusion she lifted up her key chain and said, "My mom is in recovery too." She also had one of the wide tear shaped keychain with a big N and an A on it.

Awwww Damn! As much as I was trying to keep my secret, I had been advertising that my mother was on drugs the entire time. This girl was so proud of this, I couldn't understand it. But then again, she did say recovery. My mother wasn't actually recovering she was going in and out of rehab for cool off periods and then she was right back at it. Maybe her mother was staying off drugs and if that was so then that is something to be happy about, but if she was anything like my mother she needed to take that keychain off so no one else founds out her momma was a crackhead.

Dr. Kisha Roberts Tabb

10 THE PASSING…

> "Ain't nobody perfect, everybody's hurting…"
>
> *-Koryn Hawthrone*

It was the summer of my seventh-grade year. I had completely emerged myself into my Hyde Park life. Within one year, I had become very popular in my new school. I was so popular that many of my school friends would come to my neighborhood to play. I spent my days at cheerleading practice and my evening on 45th Street. I had managed to keep my secret. I'm sure my friends wondered why I lived with my father and wondered where my mother was. Thank God they never asked. I couldn't quite figure out what I would tell them if they asked.

With the exception of a few long stints on punishment, everything had been going well.

My sister had transferred to Lincoln and I was at Louis Wirth. We had done our best to get as far away from anyone who knew my mom and more so anyone who knew she was our mom, until that summer evening while playing outside Grandma Annabell's house. Out of the corner of my eye, I see a lady and a man both walking very fast. The lady's small build reminded me of her. *No, it couldn't be her. What would she be doing all the way over here?* The closer she got, the more apparent it became she just didn't look like my mother, it was Tanya Lynn in the flesh. I was in the park along with everyone else on the block. Unbeknownst to me, my sister had also seen the end of our secret life approaching. We looked at each other and then across the street at her. Her strides had become so quick that she went from the end of the block to crossing the street right in front of us. "God please let her walk the other way. Please don't let her call my name. Maybe she doesn't see us.

Maybe if I act like I'm deep into this game of Piggy she will not notice me." I immediately thought of my sister. Would she be so happy to see her that she would run up to her in front of everyone? When I looked at her face I saw that she wanted to keep her a secret as much as I did. We hadn't seen her in months and now I knew why. She looked horrible. Her face looked so sunken in. Those high cheekbones that I asked God to bless me with all my life were so profound that it made her look like a skeleton. Her hair was cut in a short afro that looked as if it hadn't been combed or brushed in weeks. The dark cast that covered her face made me question if it was really her or if I was in the middle of a nightmare. She was walking and talking the whole time which allowed me to see that her front tooth was chipped or missing. Either way, it would give these kids so much ammunition. Why would she come over here? If she wanted to see us why wouldn't she just call us and ask us to come to 35th?

The closer she got, the thicker the air became. Who was this dude she was with and why the hell would she bring him over here? Is this who she had been with for the last few months? Is he the reason we hadn't seen her. The reason I had gone to my grandmother to ask if she was dead. Although I was pissed like hell that she had come over here to expose us, I was also so relieved that she was alive. With so many thoughts filling my mind and so little time, I didn't know what I should do. My first instinct was to run in the opposite direction but that would cause too much attention and prompt her to call my name. Before I knew it my sister was standing next to me and without words, we began to walk toward her. At least when she did say something to us no one else would hear her, we could still play it off. No one has to know she is our mother. Finally, I had a plan we would keep it brief and then go into the house that way no one could ask us any questions. We arrived in the middle of the street at the same time. It seemed as if time had been suspended, the ball seemed to hover in midair. There was no laughter. All I could hear was my heartbeat. As we approached each other my eyes said please forgive me and please keep walking. The excitement in her eyes quickly turned into shame. We passed each other only exchanging looks. I was so consumed with the discovery that was about to be made that I didn't even notice that my sister hadn't said a word either. We passed each other like strangers in the night and our secret was safe. At least for now.

Dr. Kisha Roberts Tabb

11 THE RESULTS

By Arriana Misher

"Three letters took him to his final resting place"

TLC, 1994

ately, I haven't been feeling normal. Maybe I'm sick. No, I don't mean like a cold. This would be the longest cold I've ever experienced. But no really, it's different this time. The other doctor I went to kept telling me I had pneumonia, but that doesn't sound right. I wake up in the middle of the night DRENCHED in sweat. No, I don't mean like I had a bad dream or something. It's different this time. I know my body and this just isn't right. I had a feeling that I should go to the doctor and maybe they could give me an answer. As I'm being tested so many thoughts are running through my mind. Maybe it's something extremely serious. Maybe I'm dying, or maybe not. Maybe it's nothing serious at all. Maybe I do have a cold that's just lasting super long. I don't know. I think I'm just overreacting. The last thing that would have crossed my mind was HIV.

The nervous chills that covered my body as a million other thoughts circled my brain. How would I tell everyone the news? What would be their reaction? What would be MY reaction? Here I am with the results. NO. This couldn't be possible! He was the only person I had ever been with. How could he have done this to me? He told me I was the only one for him and that he loved me. Clearly, I've been betrayed. Now I guess it's time to wipe the tears off my face because these are the cards I've been dealt. Here in my body is this sickness and here in my hand are these pills. This is real. This was my life.

12 THE DREAMS

"When I was young me and my momma had beef..."

-Tupac, 1995

I can remember it so clearly. I had spent the entire day with my momma. She had been so upset, everyone was upset, it was clear that someone had passed away. I felt honored that my momma had allowed me to comfort her because she would usually turn to my sister for that. I was determined not to leave her side. Although I remember a sense of confusion I also remember being very upset as well. Someone had died. I wasn't sure who, but whoever it was, I grieved for them. I cried and could physically feel the pain of the loss. Momma didn't say anything but it didn't bother me I was just glad to be with her, I didn't let her out of my sight.

During the days between the death and the funeral, I could smell the food that people had dropped off. I didn't understand why people brought so much food when there was a death in the family. As far as I could see, grief didn't make you hungry. The one person that I don't recall being around was my Uncle JoJo. He and momma were joined at the hip, so he had to have been the one who had passed away. I remember preparing for the services, arriving at the funeral home, lining up two at a time, my momma by my side. The family precession began. I walked the middle aisle arms - in - arm with momma. A feeling of terror spreading with each step we took. By the time we reached the end of the aisle, I was drenched in sweat and felt like my throat was closing up. I couldn't understand why I was reacting this way. I loved my Uncle JoJo, but I had been to funerals before. I looked down at the body lying in the coffin. It was Momma. Screaming, I looked at to my right. It was my sister who was attached to me. Then I woke up. Every night it was the same thing. No matter what time I went to bed I was woken up by the same kind of dream. There were several variations of this dream but the outcome was always the same - my mother was dead. The strange part of the whole thing is that in real life I had not spent much time alone with my momma. It was always the three of us, my momma, my sister and me. But in every single dream, it was just me and my momma.

One dream in particular haunted me for years to come. My momma had been in the hospital, I arrived at her room. Her motionless body lay on the bed. The only thing that continued to move was her eyes. Momma searched the room with her eyes as if surveying who was there. She stared at the wall in front of her where a crucifixion hung on the wall. Then she began to shift her body, she tapped the bed and motioned for me to sit down, I complied.

Momma laid her head on my chest and I began to stroke her hair. Like every dream before that she died, this time with her head on my chest and my hand in her hair. I would wake up and tell my sister about the dreams. Eventually, my dad found out and he wanted me to go talk to someone but I thought that was a stupid idea. It was just a dream. Whenever I would talk to my sister about it she had a telling look on her face as if she had the answer but didn't have the words. One morning before I left for school my sister left a note on the table addressed to me. It read:

Kisha,
You should talk to momma about your
dreams,
Kim

Talk to momma and say what? *Please stop getting high because I keep dreaming that you are going to die?* The truth is we are all going to die one day and I had never heard of anyone od'ing from crack cocaine. Besides, it was just a dream, or so I thought.

Dr. Kisha Roberts Tabb

13 THE SECRET

By Dr. Kimyona Roberts

"Searching for a reason searching for a piece of mind..."

-Miguel, 2012

I have a secret, and I can't tell nobody. Actually, I have a burden, and I don't mind bearing it. I mean, why should she have to bear it alone? Momma came to our house one night while Daddy and Kisha were sleeping. I didn't know why I was up; I was always the first one sleep. She didn't come in. She stood at the door, handed me a note and told me not to read it until she was gone. I unfolded the notebook paper and read the letter, it read "I have HIV and the doctors said I have 6 months to live." I tore the note up into little pieces as if that would undo the words it contained. I then put the pieces in an envelope and tucked it away for safekeeping. This late night interplay would dictate my actions over the next year or so. Her silence fed my silence - it said to me that she didn't want to talk about it. Her letter, addressed only to me, said that she didn't want anyone to know. It also said, "I am ashamed and you should be ashamed too." Hell, I was already ashamed of her - crack did nothing for her looks. The diagnosis itself wasn't a big surprise, lots of women on drugs were getting HIV from the men in their lives - it was the timeline.

As I pondered this new burden, I began to fancy myself as the second soldier in momma's war for her life - no wonder she only had six months. Thinking over her life and interactions with other people, I felt it only proper that she didn't want to tell anybody. Nobody in her family or mine ever had anything good to say about her. She was a crack head, whose kids pretty much moved out on their own 'cause she was so negligent. They would rip her apart if they found out. I had to protect her from further humiliation, further isolation, and further condemnation. At this point, I could care less if anyone else knew. My only concern was that she didn't tell my Kisha. I knew they didn't really get along, but dang. I think she was afraid to tell her, especially since she was afraid to actually TELL me. I don't know if momma thought she would get an attitude and have a tantrum in response to this new disappointment - I mean she does have a short fuse. Maybe she realized, like I always knew, how emotionally fragile she was, and didn't think she could handle it. The only time I ever mentioned her diagnosis aloud was when I was encouraging her to tell my sister. There was no keeping it from her, especially in light of her unspoken psychic abilities. She started having dreams that Momma died for God's sake. Sometimes it was easy to act like it wasn't happening; Momma and I never talked about it out loud. It was almost like neither one of us knew. That was until my sister woke me up and wanted to tell me about one of her many dreams. What was the greater burden, knowing momma was dying and it was nothing I could do about it or watching the effects of my secret on my sister and not be able to offer an answer to her nightmares? This secret of mine was turning me into a traitor and conspirator against my own sister. "You have to tell her," I pleaded once it became obvious the dreams weren't going away. She kept asking me what I think they mean. They're gonna drive her crazy. And it's not fair that I know and she doesn't. She's gonna be mad at when she finds out. She needed time to be nicer to Momma, so she'd have something other than arguments to remember. This could be her chance to forgive and forget. It got so bad that I once wrote a note of my own. "You should talk to Momma about your dreams." I wanted to tell her but I had to defend my momma.

My new mission in life was to be there for my mother. My new bedtime prayer didn't have anything to do with bringing me a prince charming, making me popular at school, or letting Daddy hit the lottery. My prayer now was "Lord please don't let anything happen to my mother while I'm not around, and please let Annabelle die peacefully when she is ready to go." I sometimes left Annabell out 'cause I knew she had plenty of folks praying for her and her ticket to heaven was already paid for. Well, one out of two ain't bad at least Granny died peacefully.

Dr. Kisha Roberts Tabb

14 THE INTRO

"If I'd have known Sunday morning that you would be gone,

I wouldn't ever come home

I wouldn't have answered my phone to hear the voice had

a tone, I knew that something was wrong…"

-Marsha Ambrosia, 2011

I t was a Sunday morning. Usually, I would be up getting ready for noon mass. I don't know why I was still in the bed.

The phone rang, it was my grandmother. The tone in her voice was strange, even though she was trying to sound calm it was something about the way she asked, "yall getting ready for church?" My grandmother had this way of going all around the reason she was calling so I answered each one of her questions knowing that it had nothing to do with why she called. After a million and one questions grandma finally got to why she was calling, "Peaches called, she said yo momma over there sick and need to go to the hospital."

"Over where," I asked her.

"At their house. She has been over there for the last few days. Y'all ain't heard from her?"

My sister and I got up, got dressed and jumped on the bus. When we arrived to my grandmother's house, she was on the phone with Peaches. She looked so frightened. She turned to us and said, "go over there the ambulance is on the way."

My sister and I got there just as the ambulance was going into the building. By the grace of God, the elevators were working, which was a rare occasion in the projects. When we got up to the apartment, the paramedics were strapping her to the gurney. All I could think is somebody gave her some bad stuff. When we got downstairs I went to climb in the ambulance and I heard my mom say to the medic "naw, I want my other daughter to ride with me."

"Both of them can ride with you," the paramedics informed her.

Gasping for breath she, said, "no I only want the other one to ride with me."

My heart sank into my stomach. What had I done to her? Why didn't she want me to ride with her? How am I supposed to get there?

As the ambulance drove off, I remember thinking, *what about me, what about me, who gone take me?* The more I asked the angrier I became. "Fuck her she doesn't want me there, I won't to be there."

I went from standing on the project porch with the lights and sound from the ambulance getting further and further away, to standing at the door of Mercy hospital getting my I am pissed face straight! They had already taken my mother into the back so the triage nurse escorted me back to her room. Wow, I didn't even know they had private rooms in the emergency room.   When I walked in the room my sister looked as if she was trying to apologize with her eyes. I wanted to tell her that I wasn't mad at her, but I had committed to being pissed so I had to stick with it.   As we waited for the doctor me and my sister chatted, my sister and my mom chatted, but she didn't say a word to me. For the life of me, I couldn't figure out what I had done to her. She barely looked at me.

After an hour in that room with the tension so thick you could cut it with a knife, the doctor finally arrived to examine her. She took her vitals and looked at her throat. She had a rash in her mouth that looked like the type babies get. The doctor called it thrush.   She continued to examine her and then asked, "Mrs. Roberts what medication are you taking for your HIV?"

"What did she say? For her what? Kim, what did she just ask momma? Momma, what she talking about?" No one would answer my

91

questions. It was like no one could hear me. Like no one could see the tears pouring down my face. The doctor just left as if she hadn't turned my entire world upside down. My mother looked at me and said, "That's why I didn't want you to know, you cry too much." And that's how I got introduced to HIV. Whose Little Girl am I? I am the little girl of a dying mother.

Dr. Kisha Roberts Tabb

15 MY LAST TWO CENT

"It's Over Now…"

-Kirk Franklin, 1997

I'm so tired. The days seem to get longer and longer. The pain in my body gets stronger and stronger. The meds seemed to be getting weaker and weaker. I'm trying so hard to hold on. I've lost so much weight I can barely recognize my own face in the mirror. As a little girl, I never imagined this day would come. It's taking everything that I have to drown out that calming voice that kept whispering, "Come, my child and rest." My hand is so weak I can barely write my last request but I push through.

> Please don't say that I gave up,
> just say I gave in.
> Don't say I lost the battle, for it's
> God's war to lose or win.

Dr. Kisha Roberts Tabb

Please don't say how good I was,
but that I did my best.

Just say I tried to do what's right.
To give the most I could, not do less.

Please do not give wings or halos,
that's for God to do.

I want no more than I deserve, no
extras, just my due.

Please don't give flowers, or talk in
harsh tones.

Don't be concerned about me
now, I'm well with God, I've made
it home.

Don't talk about what could have
been, it's over and done.

Just see to all my loved one's
needs, the battle has been won.

When you draw a picture of me,
don't draw me as a saint.

I've done some good, I've done
some wrong, so use all the paint.

Not just the bright and light tones,
use some gray and dark.

In fact, don't put me down on
canvas; paint me in your heart.

Whose Little Girl Am I?

Don't remember all the good
times, but remember all the bad.
For life is full of many things, some
happy and some sad.
But if you must do something, then
I have one last request,
Forgive me for the wrong that I've
done and with the love that's left,
Thank God for my soul resting,
Thank God for all who love me,
Praise God who loves me best

-Author unknown

Whose Little girl, am I? Right now, I only belong
to God.

Dr. Kisha Roberts Tabb

16 THE LOST ONE

This is dedicated to Keytoria Roberts 1982

Everybody keeps asking each other if they are ok. Why do people ask such stupid questions? I don't know how I'm feeling. I'm anxious, scared a little, and a little excited! The last thing I remember Momma saying was not to mind what people may say about her.

Everyone is doing a whole lot of whispering and closing the doors behind them. I know they talking about Momma. I guess I wasn't really surprised when I heard them say she had passed. She was always in the hospital, sometimes for a few days and sometimes for a few weeks. She would be fine one day, a cold the next and would end up back in the hospital.

The preacher kept saying we know not the time nor the hour. All I know is Momma went into the hospital Monday night and now one week later they have laid her to rest and everyone's sitting in grandma's living room in their Easter clothes, asking each other if they are ok. I wonder if any of them asked Momma if she was ok. Everybody is talking about Momma, her beautiful smile, her sense of humor, and how much fun she was. If she was so much fun I wonder how come they never went to the hospital when Momma was there.

The preacher said if you don't get right with God then you won't make it into heaven. I hope Momma got right with God. The lady from the help center where Momma use to go spoke and said that she was smiling down. If that's true she must be in heaven. She had a red ribbon pinned to her dress just like the one Momma wore. Momma's friends from the help center were always so nice, they always asked momma if she was ok. Momma said that they were people from her community. Come to think of it, they all had red ribbons too. They were weird too though. They always used letters that didn't spell anything. They all spelled the same words azt –aazzztt that's not a word. And hiv-hhiivv. What kind of word is that? I guess it was their own little language that they only spoke in their community. I know my sisters are sad and will miss Momma, but they had a lot more time with her than I did, that is until now. I love seeing them but I have to leave grandma's house and go find Momma. I have so much to show her. I know we have an eternity to catch up, but it's been so long. I can't wait to find her so I can show her all around heaven.

Dr. Kisha Roberts Tabb

17 THE FIRST TIME

"I'm nervous and I'm tremblin' waitin' for you to walk in. I'm trying hard to relax but I just can't keep still…"

-Betty Wright, 1974

I t is 3:15. In an hour my whole life will be changed. Oh my God, I hope I know what to do. OK let me set the mood. Room cleaned, all our pictures are propped up, and my "Michel'le" CD is set to the second track. Where is the remote? I want to make sure that the song comes on at just the right time. Oh my God is that the bell? Is this really happening? I wonder if he can tell how nervous I am.

He came in and we headed straight upstairs. This is the first time he's been in my room. I'd never noticed how immature this room is. I'm sure he thinks I'm a lame for real. He's obviously not looking at the décor because we could barely get in the room good and he was kissing me. This is really happening. We'd been kissing for what seemed like an eternity. All I can think about is whether I shaved under my arms or not, and are my toe nails polished. The longer we kissed, the more nervous I got.

Whose idea was this anyway?

We seem to be on two different planets because he's doing a whole lot of heavy breathing and my heart is beating so fast I can hardly breathe. Why is he asking me if I'm ok? Can he tell I scared?

"Yeah, I'm good."

We went right back into our passionate kissing session, and all of a sudden, I feel him pulling my shirt up.

I wonder if this the right time to press play?

As my shirt comes over my head, I press play.

Now Michel'le is singing "somethings in my heart, something in my heart."

103

He must like this song as much as I do because now his body is moving to the beat of the song.

When did he get so much rhythm?

The music is helping me calm down, and now I'm moving to the beat. Now I freeze again cause he pulling on my jeans. The voices in my head are screaming stop but everything else is saying keep going, so we do. Since this is clearly going to happen, I might as well let nature take its course. Now I'm thinking how much I love him, there is no one else I'd rather give this gift to than him. Finally, I'm ready. He's kissing all the right places. I could care less about anything other than what's happening at this moment. Between moans, I whispered in his ear, "get the condom."

"What do you mean you forgot them?... So, what are we supposed to do without a condom?... No, you can't just put it in ... No, you can't pull out...oooohhhhh boy, stop."

Dr. Kisha Roberts Tabb

18 NO NEW FRIENDS

"No foes, real friends, we ain't even have to pretend"

The Carter's, 2018

I must admit high school was hard and the students were cruel. I began high school with a ready-made crew. We had all went to junior high school together and believed that we were indestructible. We had spent nearly every weekend together since the 6th grade and new each other's deepest secrets. We added a few members to our junior high cohort and the crew was formed.

I thought that these would be my girls forever, forever lasted all of freshmen year. By the time we made it to the tenth-grade secrets had been told, relationships had been ruined, sides had been picked, and our unbreakable bonds had been shattered. When all the sides had been picked, I felt like an outcast. I had managed to hold on to Rea, who was actually one of the new members of our crew. She did not attend junior high with us but if you observed us you would have never known. I knew it was rough on her because she was caught in the middle, still friends with them and still maintained her friendship with me. Although sometimes I wanted her to just pick a side, even at 15 I knew that wasn't fair.

For the first few months of school, I went back and forth regarding my four-year friendship with these girls. At some point, I decided that I had enough. I still remained friends with Rea but decided that the whole "crew" thing was just not for me. I began to walk alone through the hallways and for the first time since I could remember I was cool with that.

Kenwood had so many activities, I could tell Rea was having a hard time dividing herself between them and me. I decided to go to the basketball pep rally alone. As I approached the bleachers I asked an unfamiliar face if anyone was sitting next to her.

"You are now," she said and laughed.

I had never seen this girl before but she had such a welcoming spirit. I sat down next to her. We laughed and joked the entire pep rally. I didn't know it, but I had met one of my best friends that day. From that day forward, we were inseparable. We were in different divisions, shared no classes, no extra-curricular activities, yet we were always together. Besides Natia, Neka was the only other person that I shared my secret with. She cut classes to go to the doctor with me and my mother. My mother had to have a spinal tap but I had a final exam and Kim also had a school commitment. Best friend to the rescue, she left school lied and told the doctors she was me and, held my mother's hand during her spinal tap. You often hear people say that you meet your lifelong friends in college. Yes, I did Dekeila, Michelle, Tucora and Ebony, but the unbreakable bonds that were developed in the halls of Kenwood were irreplaceable. The experiences I have shared with Ardi, Kisha, Malinda, Nneka, Rea, and Toni, no one else would ever understand or even believe if we told them. This was My Crew, no judgment. We all came from different backgrounds but no one cared, we had each other's back.

Like any other crew, there were members who were closer to some than others, but for me, these are the six women that got me through all my break-ups, celebrated my accomplishments, laughed at my flaws, held me down through tragedy, and took some of the pressure off Natia.

As life would have it, I would develop some amazing friendships, a work family and sister/friends. I always say if you don't have friends like mine, I feel sorry for you. When life has thrown its toughest punches at me, I have had a village of amazing women to catch me dust me off and send me on my way. When I look back over my accomplishments I have had my very own cheer squad to back me up. The next time you hear a woman say that women are too messy, let them know that they have the wrong friends.

If you are lacking a Natia who will never let you feel sorry for yourself while getting you right together with a smile, your best friend needs work. If you don't have a Neka who would hold you down a thousand miles away and crack a joke during your most embarrassing snotty cries, you have the wrong best friend. If your girl is not available to ride down on anyone and have never missed one event since the ninth grade, then you need a Toni. If you don't require much but need a friend that you don't have to talk to every day but know when you need her she is right there, Dekeila is your girl. If you are lacking a prayer worrier who will bring the Bible out while the plane seems to be descending mid-flight, I must introduce you to Ebony. If you don't have a group of ladies that you can meet on the first day of a new job and develop a friendship that will take you through 15 years of deaths, graduations, birthdays, new relationships breakups and growing kids then you are lacking a Kelly, Marvene, and Tasha. I can't forget the "we can do anything" friend, who will hype you up to start a business, buy the house, build a brand and travel the world. If she's not part of your circle, you're missing a Michon. If you don't have a ride or die like Niecy, who is down for whatever while wearing four-inch heels, and the most fabulous outfit you've ever seen, then you have no idea what you are missing. So we all need that what do you need and will go above and beyond to get it done friend, well I have Jeannie. Then, there's the friend who will walk right up to you and say "You know you acting a fool, now what's going on with you." If you don't have that keep it a buck friend, then you need a Tamar. Every girl needs big sister/friends that act as sounding boards, shout out to Sherri, Jen-Jen, and Baby Dee. Now I am not one to brag but these beauties that make up my Squad are the bomb. With girls like this who needs new friends.

Dr. Kisha Roberts Tabb

19 THE CHURCH GIRL

"When I think about Jesus. What He's done for me. When I think about Jesus.
How he set me free..."

-Kirk Franklin, 1996

To live in my grand-momma's house you had to be saved sanctified and filled with the Holy Spirit, accepting Jesus Christ as your Lord and Savior. So that's exactly what we all did. We went to church seven days a week. Monday night was revival. Tuesday was 5 am prayer. Wednesday night was Bible Study. Thursday Grandma had choir rehearsal. Friday evening was youth service. Saturday we attended the Church meetings. And Sunday we attended 3 services and ate dinner. I guess she thought if we were in the church, we were safe. So we obliged, not that we were ever given a choice.

In elementary and high school, I couldn't go nowhere and I couldn't do nothing. If I wasn't at church or with somebody from church, I couldn't do it. I guess in my Grandma's mind, the church kept us from all the worldly stuff that was going on outside the walls of the church. As much as I resented the fact that I couldn't do anything, I found it hilarious while momma was spending so much time keeping us safe from "worldly" things, she never checked to see how many "worldly" people were in the church. Before long, I didn't even mind going. Hell, by the time I turned 15 I had done more dirt in the church than all my worldly friends. Church activities offered a sanctuary for experimentation. I learned at an early age that a cute light skinned girl with long hair could get just about anything she wanted from a man.

And I do mean any man. From the altar boys to the Senior Pastor.

My Grandma had me on such a short leash, church along with school became my refuge. I looked forward to school because I knew that good grades was my ticket out of Grandma's house. The scholarships started pouring in, and grandma was so proud. I don't think she realized how far out of her reach I would be once I went away to college. I remember my first day on campus, I watched her drive away and I remember thinking, *this is freedom!*

I fit right in at UAPB. The southern boys loved me and my cute face, small waist, long hair don't care attitude. I had the whole campus on lock. I loved me a country man; actually country men. I controlled the scene, I answered the phone when I wanted to and, only called when I wanted to get some. I always wanted to get some. I didn't care what people thought of me, this was my body and I could give it to whomever I want to, as much as I wanted to. Not like with Elder Brosewell, who controlled when and how often we did it. Grandma didn't have a clue what was going on in the back of that church, when I was "helping out." Well now I help myself to whatever man I want, only when I want to. I could get any man I want, so why not.

20 Ex-Factor

I may not have been the finest thing walking but I was for damn sure the most loyal. I believed that when you loved someone you stood by them "no matter what." No matter what. What did that mean? For me, it meant dirty looks as I rode in the car with him. It meant not hearing from him all day and, bam, getting a late-night call asking, "What you doing?" I already knew that meant "I'm coming to get you." My no matter what meant walking down the street and seeing him drive by with another woman in the car, receiving a phone call two days before I left for college informing me that

118

she was having his baby, allowing him to convince me that she was lying, and spending my first weekend in college laid up with him while the Que's was having a welcoming party for incoming students. My no matter what included rushing home in the middle of finals to be by his side through the loss of his mother, only to have him leave me at his house for hours, returning with a card from his baby momma and unborn child.

"I keep letting you back in, how can I explain myself..." -Lauryn Hill, 1998

I'm sure to the outside world I looked like a fool, but it didn't matter to me as long as I looked loyal in his eyes. So, I continued to operate in my No Matter What world. Each time accepting more and more. Using my school refund check to buy his new daughter Christmas gifts, staying in the house every weekend to babysit his son while he left and came back at the crack of dawn, being informed by his son that she was at

119

my door, choosing to stay in the bed, knowing that if I had gotten up I would have killed him and her. The endless phone calls and pop-ups from her. I believed his explanation that she was just jealous of us. My no matter what included sheer embarrassment when my co-worker at AT&T placed her call on hold to show me that she had a telephone account in his name at her address.

"As painful as this thing has been, I just can't see myself with no one else..." -Lauryn Hill, 1998

After years of the back and forth, him in and out of the house I realize I am pregnant. I can't imagine not keeping it, but what the hell am I gon' do with a baby. Will it change things? At this point it doesn't matter, my baby is coming and I can't worry about what he gon' do. I have to do what I have to do. He did change for a minute, but before I could get used to the new him he was gone and I was still carrying his baby. He decided that he no longer wanted to live with me. He needed some space and was going to stay with his aunt. On a late-night drive, I see his car parked right in front of the door of a high-rise apartment building. My heart dropped down to my stomach and the pain it caused would not allow me to remain in the car. I walked in, went to the tenant directory and there was her name.

I rung the bell and his voice rang out, "Who is it?" I couldn't believe it.

He had left me five months pregnant to move in with her. "Does she know you about to have a baby?" I responded.

"You about to have a baby?" *Wow, this is what I get for my no matter what? Ok, I'll show his ass; no matter what.*

This time no matter what included me throwing brick after brick at his car, setting off the alarm causing him to come down, making him my new target. He managed to get pass me and get into the car. Oh, but I was gone show his ass no matter what. I chased him, ramming into the back of his car, pushing him out into oncoming trafficking. This is what I had been reduced too, a crazy baby momma doing anything to be validated and recognized. This is too much.

> *"You let go and I'll let go too. No one's hurt me more than you and no one ever will..." -*
> *Lauryn Hill., 1998*

Dr. Kisha Roberts Tabb

21 THE BLESSING

> "Unsure what the balance held, I touched my belly overwhelmed by what I had been chosen to perform..."
>
> *-Lauryn Hill, 1998*

The events of this weekend are those moments in life that make you strong. With everything that is going on with my grandmother and work, now my Mae wants to test me. All I want is to help her become the young lady she was created to be. Not sure if I am upset with her or with myself, I wonder where I went wrong. I constantly ask myself "Am I overreacting? Is this normal?" I wouldn't know because I didn't have a guide. I think about how I had wished my mother was active in my life when I was her age. I look at Mae and I see such beautiful potential. I still remember the day that I found out that I was carrying her. As scared as I was, the secret joy that I felt was overwhelming. So many thoughts had been going through my head as I walked to Walgreens on my lunch break. I don't even think I had missed my period yet, my body just felt different. I had been sick for a few days but it didn't feel like stomach flu. My breast was sore and heavy. Being that this was not my first rodeo, I recognized the signs before I had noticed that my menstrual was late. Arriving back at the office, my first stop was the washroom. Minutes after entering the room began spinning I couldn't believe that this was happening. How was I going to tell my Dad? My relationship is not in a great place, this is not an ideal time to bring a child into this mess. Yet from the moment I saw the two blue lines, I knew that I would be keeping my baby. The thought of doing anything else never even crossed my mind. From that day forward, I began to plan for this new life coming up with two names one for a girl and one for a boy. I prayed that I would be a better mother than what I had. Although I wanted a boy, when I found out I was having a girl I adjusted my crown and began to create her tiara. God had blessed me with my very own princess. I was determined to keep her from ever feeling abandoned, unloved, unsupported. I wanted her to know that I had prepared for her entry, I set the stage and had everything prepared for months before she made her entry.

I had been laboring 44 hours and was praying again, "Lord please save my baby girl, don't let her die." I could see the look of pure terror on everyone's face in the room. The cheering minutes prior as the crown of her head appeared turned into silence once she had arrived. I heard code blue and the doctors swarm the plastic bassinet that she had been placed in. I waited to hear her cry but it never came. I had seen in the movies how happy new mothers were to hear the cry of their newborn child. I waited and waited, no cry. I only heard the wheels begin to roll as they took my baby girl to the NICU. As hard as it was to leave my baby girl in the hospital after I had been released I continued to prepare for her homecoming. Finally, the day had arrived and I remember how afraid I was bringing her home. Everything that I had learned in childbirth class, a parenting course, the books I read, it all went out the window. I could not remember a thing. I had this beautiful baby in my arms and had no idea what to do with her.

"Pardon the way that I stare. There's nothing else to compare. The sight of you leaves me weak. There are no words left to speak..." -Lauryn Hill, 1998

Again, I began to pray,

"Lord please teach me how to be her mother. Equip me with everything I need to care for this precious gift you have blessed me with and God please keep me from messing her up."

22 RAISING A QUEEN

"I thank you for choosing me to come through unto life to be a beautiful reflection of his grace…"

-Lauryn Hill, 1998

A t 21 years old I hadn't accomplished much of anything. I had dropped out of school and I was working a job I hated. However, I had a chance to make my mark on the world. I had been given the greatest opportunity of my life. I had been given a second chance. I promised God the day she was born that if he spared her life I would be the best mother I could be. I didn't care what I had to do; I would give my daughter everything that I had. Although I didn't have the mother I wanted, I did remember how it felt to have a mother's love. That love was the one thing that I chased, longed for, and was never able to get back once I lost it. My daughter would never know what that felt like. I would love her with every ounce of my being. I would give her everything I wanted from my mother. I would protect and keep her safe from harm.

Early on I realized that I had been given a task that was like nothing I had ever experienced. From the moment she could speak I could recognize that she was gifted. Nothing was ever hard for her. When she was just weeks old, I removed the pacifier from her mouth and she never missed it. Days after her 1st birthday, I laid her down and took the bottle from her mouth. She cried for a few minutes and never requested a bottle again. She was potty trained two weeks after being introduced to the concept. It was like she said a few words then before you knew it she was speaking in complete sentences. At the age of three, she was using words like "actually." By four, she would use adjectives like "mysterious. "

Upon returning from my time in Africa, the first thing I did was to apply for her to attend New Concept, an Afrocentric school. I had heard some amazing things about this school. After being in Normal, IL for the first four years of her life, it was important that she learned in an environment that celebrated her culture as well as her academic ability. Shortly after applying we got the call. I immediately called her dad so he could be sure to get the day off. My daughter and I arrived before her dad and were called right in for the interview and test. Before the test, the principal began to speak to Mae but she didn't respond. Wanting to see where this was going, I fell back. After two more times of attempting to engage her the principal spoke to me, "I see this one has a problem listening."

Before I could respond Mae said, "I'm sorry are you talking about me?"

Slower than she had been speaking before, the principal said, "yes little girl I have spoken to you several times and you weren't listening to a thing I said."

Mae looked at me and then at the principle with a confused expression and said, "I was listening, but I don't understand Spanish."

The principal explained that she was not speaking Spanish she just speaks with an accent. Mae responded to this new information very apologetic and said, "I'm sorry but I don't speak accent either, I only know how to speak English."

Unable to control herself the principle began to laugh. She proceeded with the test. Once they had finished and she escorted Mae out to me and said to me, "This one here is very smart she answered every question correctly. We would love to have her."

Before I could speak she turned to Mae and said, "You are a very intelligent young lady but by your own account you can only speak English, I can speak your English and my own native language, so who do you think is smarter?"

My child looked up, thought about the question and then said, "Actually I think I may be a little smarter because I told you I only speak English but you keep speaking accent."

This was the kind of kid I was raising.

I also noticed early on that she was strong-willed. If she did not want to do something, she just wouldn't do it, and that was all to it. I remember having her tested for a gifted program; the time of the test conflicted with my work schedule so my dad took her. Excited to see how she did I called my dad several times; when I was able to get him I could tell by the tone of his voice things didn't go well. "Well, she wasn't feeling it." I learned later that she refused to answer any of the questions that were being asked. At the time disappointed I now know that everything happens for a reason and for Jaylah her foundation years were best served at a charter school not far from my grandmother's home which is where she would spend each day after school. My daughter and my grandmother had a very special relationship and she poured into my Mae daily. In retrospect, my daughter's personality and discipline were highly influenced by the rigorous structures at school and her time at Granny's. I look at the young woman who stands before me and I am so grateful for the efforts of the village that raised her. She makes some of the most profound statements and I can usually hear the whisper of a village member behind her words.

Now don't get me wrong, between the ages of 11 and 14 I thought that someone had broken into my home and switched my daughter with an alien that I did not recognize nor understood. She didn't seem to care much about school, my opinion, or anyone else's for the matter. There was always one person that she never wanted to disappoint, and that was

Granny.   Unfortunately, Granny had been snatched away from Mae by Alzheimer's. Again members of the village began to step in - Ms. Barbara, my sisters, my dad, Mr. Tabb and her G-ma. I had reached a point where I didn't know what else to do so we tried family counseling. Our sessions became discussions between Mae and the counselor about who was a better Jazz singer, Nina Simone or Ella Fitzgerald. Each session ending with the counselor telling me how intelligent and articulate she was. We never got around to why she refused cleaning her room, read her winter break books, and never wanted to talk about what was bothering her; so we ended the rap sessions between Mae and the counselor.   I remember when my sister lost her mind Granny saying she was "giving her back to God" so I decided that I would do the same with Mae. I began to pray not just for her but for me to be an example that she could follow. I prayed for her protection and more than anything I prayed that God would return the daughter I once knew. Delayed never meant denied because before long I was able to see glimpses of the daughter I prayed for, but she was still not the same girl that I remembered. Mae once told me "My mother was not on drugs she was here for me, so I don't need the same things that you needed. I got my mother." She had emerged an amazing, confident, intelligent, insightful young woman that knew who and whose she was. God had remembered my original prayer not to mess her up, so he decided to give me a double portion. The Queen that was produced was one with more attributes than I could ever have dreamed or imagined.

23 ADJUSTING MY CROWN

By Jaylah Roberts-Coleman

"I keep her hair braided brought her a black Barbie; I keep her mind free she ain't no black zombie..."

-Jean Grae/Talib Kweli, 2004

What can I say?

Being the daughter of Kisha Roberts-Tabb, correction: Dr. Kisha Roberts-Tabb hasn't been easy. Being a Roberts, you have to live up to that name; we've got all types of doctors in the family. MD, Ph.D., Ed.D., you name it. So, no, I cannot relate to my peers who have no goals and are content with having a minimum wage 9 to 5. I need more. But I wouldn't know that if I didn't have a great example living under the same roof.

Even when things got in her way, my mother still finished. Two of her degrees took longer than expected, but she still put everything into it. She still came out on top with good relationships with professors that would later become good resources that she still keeps in contact with. I mean it's hard to not love my mom. Truth be told, I sometimes think her likability is my least favorite attribute of hers. Of course, everyone wants a cool mom, but I had to learn how to share her. All of my friends like to call her "Ma" and at first, I was not having it. The first person to try this was my friend Ariel. She used to call her "Ma" all the time and I'd get visibly upset. I was her ONLY child. So I'd nicely tell Ariel to stop calling her Ma, and I'd tell my mom to stop responding to it. Funny enough, now my mom has at least 5 children, who all call her "Ma."

I could share a lot of things, but my mom and my granny were not up for grabs. I was her only great-grandchild, and I loved it. We were so close and I could tell her anything. I could also depend on her to save me from my mom. Even to the point that she'd tell my mother to leave her house, but without me. I can admit she spoiled me, but not with material things. Her love was enough. I was her baby and that never changed. Until her last breath, I was still her baby, and I was still by her side as I was when I was a child.

Another truth: I held a small grudge against my mother when my granny died. It was a few days before my senior year started. Orientation was the next day, but my granny was in hospice. I wasn't going to go to orientation; I was going to stay with her like I had been for the past few days. I hadn't been home while she was in hospice, I just had my mom bring me clothes and food. I couldn't leave, I had to be there for her like she was my entire life. But my mother told me I should go to my senior orientation, she said I could come right back afterwards. After much debate, I agreed and went home that night. A couple of hours later we got a call to come back to the hospital, and I knew it wasn't good. When we arrived I already knew, I just had a bad feeling. And as I suspected, she was no longer with us. I was so upset because I told her I'd be there. And my mother knew, she knew I was mad at her. It took me a while to get over that, and I had to work that out with myself.

We became closer after that because she was the next closest thing I had. I had to understand that she only wanted the best for me, and she was trying to get my mind off of the situation at hand. Now we have an understanding, and I can say that she is honestly one of my closest friends. She had always been one of my favorite people, but it was different now. Especially since I've been in college, we talk almost every day sometimes more than once a day. And yes, my friends in college call her "Ma" and "Auntie." If you're wondering, I'm definitely okay with that.

24 MY LANE

"So Gone Baby Gone Baby Don't Be Long, I know you have to get your hustle on..."

-Erykah Badu, 2010

My grandma always said that looks could get 'em but you have to do a whole lot more to keep 'em. I was really good at get 'em but keeping them was another story. I may not have known it all but I knew how to catch me a baller. Basketballer! Footballer! Hoodballer! They kept me fly and I kept them high. Tray would say I was like heroin one hit and nigga was hooked. That is until the next pretty young thing let him hit it.

"I know you got to get your hustle on..." -Erykah Badu, 2010

Now they would play in the streets but they always came home to momma, and momma was always home waiting. Hell, my grandma said that everything had a price, and all them extra hoes were the price I had to pay for the lifestyle I was living. Now don't get it twisted, I wasn't no punk. I went through phones, checked emails, GPS systems, would follow a nigga and didn't hesitate to ask about every page, text, and tweet. Every one of them was the same man with a different name, Ray, Shawn, Reggie, and Hakim. They all had deep pockets, big appetites, and wanted way more than they could handle. They all thought they were brand new, but like grandma always said "it ain't nothing new under the sun... ain't nothing you can do that ain't already been done." As long as they kept paying I sat back and let them keep playing. I played my role and stayed in my lane. Every night was the same: Where you at? Who you wit? Where have you been? What time are you coming home? It was like we were playing a game, I asked, they lied, I knew it, and still, I made myself available to them every night. Each time giving a little more, as if I was auditioning for a permanent role in their lives. And each night when the curtain closed I knew that I had given just enough to make sure that the next night he would end up back in my bed and not hers. Yea this was a game and I was in it to win it. I hit all the right spots, kissed all the right places and said all the right things. Shit if I was going down it would not be for lack of effort. I was wifey, a lady in the streets and a freak in the sheets. I knew that every woman in his contact list was jockeying for my position. Shawn stayed on the road so I knew he had a jump off in every city so when he came home I always put it down. Reggie had six kids and six baby mommas and doubled Tray's six-figure salary. There was no way I was gone be number seven, besides they had the babies and I had the crib. Now, Hakim, he was a hustler turned record executive. The federal bid he did kept "his street cred" in check way after he left

142

the game. He always promised to make an honest woman out of me. Bullshit! The first night we met he said, "girl you gon' be my wife" now four years later I'm still just "wifey." With Hakim anything goes, he loves to experiment. At least he is honest he likes variety and has never apologized for it. What was I gone do? He was paid. He was good. Truth be told I loved him. It didn't hurt that he was paid! So like the rest with Hakim, I played the game, every night was the same: Where you at? Who you wit? Where have you been? What time are you coming home? I asked he lied, I knew it, and still, I made myself available to him every night. I knew there was a price to pay for this lifestyle I just never knew it would cost so much. It's so funny all the questions I've asked men throughout my life, yet I've never questioned my own worth, would that make them think I'm insecure.

25 SWEET THANG

"My skin is tan. My hair is fine. My hips invite you, my mouth like wine..."

-Nina Simone, 1966

What you see now may be Facebook, Instagram, and Snap Chat worthy but the journey here has been hard as hell. I hear the whispering and all of the chatter about what I do. I often wonder where all of these opinions were when my mamma's man was messing with me. How many of these people who are so appalled by the work I do were just as outraged when my neighbor raped me? I do what I got to do to pay these bills. You think I enjoy lying under these nasty men, feeling their sweat drip down on me with every thrust into my flesh?

When I was little I wanted to be a public speaker, a dancer, and a lawyer. I have always been able to command a crowd. I always got good grades, my teachers told me I could be anything that I wanted to be. I even got a scholarship to one of the top private high schools in the nation. My grandma told me I should go, but I didn't know anyone there, it was so far and there were no black kids, so I decided to go to the neighborhood school. It was there where I met the love of my life Meech, he was so nice, came from a good family too. He played ball, went to church and his grades were alright. I mean he wasn't as smart as me but he did ok. We got along so well I could be myself around him. No airs, just silly ole me. Meech had a way of making me feel like I was the only person in the world. Even though he was two years ahead of me we were able to have the most profound conversations.

The summer he left for college I was so happy for him because he had gotten his ticket out of the hood, but at the same time, I couldn't believe he was leaving me. At first, we wrote to each other all the time. Meech's letters were filled with stories of weekend parties and dorm room shenanigans. That year I lived for Christmas break because I would get to see him, hear his voice, and feel his touch. Finally, December was here. I even welcomed the snow because it was my confirmation that my love would be home soon. At last, he was home and we had so many plans. We spent the first night with his family; although I wanted Meech all to myself I was happy just being in his presence. The next day we had planned to go to the drive-in movie, so when the phone beeped I figured it was Meech telling me he was on his way. Instead, it was Tammy, Meech's cousin. When I answered the phone I could barely understand her, I was able to make out "they shot him, he's gone." He's gone. "Who's gone?"

After losing Meech nothing else really mattered. Following Meech's death, I suffered from depression, I didn't want to do anything. I stopped going to school. The idea of leaving the house was daunting. Eventually, I did leave the house and the world outside seemed like it was swallowing me whole. I thought I would never love again, but then I met Slim.

Slim was the complete opposite of Meech. I think that's what made me notice him. I figured because he was so different, I could never love him the way I loved Meech, which meant I wouldn't miss him as much when he left. Slim's entire family were all GDs. Slim was all about his paper, so he sold weed which had become my way of coping since losing Meech. He spent a little money too so it was definitely worth my time. It wasn't like I had anything else to do; I hadn't been to school in two years. I was 17 yrs. old, no job, no school, so no future. Before I knew it I was spending every minute of the day with Slim. I accompanied him to all his deliveries, even made a few out of town runs with him. I was his ride or die, at least that's what he called me. Six months later I realized that I had fallen for him hard. Now he was all that I knew Slim, Slim, and more Slim. It didn't matter what my Grandma said, Tammy or anyone else. Unless Slim said it, it didn't mean shit to me. When Slim started tripping about the block being dry and how it wasn't no money out there, I couldn't help but notice how the lack of income was affecting our relationship. Slim had become hard to be around but like any ride or die, I couldn't kick him while he was down. So I stayed and bore the brunt of his frustration. The day that he told me he had a business proposal for me, a business deal where we could be equal partners, I was excited to hear what he had in mind. "What? I ain't nobodies hoe!" At first, Slim laughed and said, "Calm down Ma I'm just fucking with you." But in reality, he was dead serious and he brought it up every chance he got. He talked about how much money we could make. He said it would be so easy like taking candy from a baby. According to Slim I didn't have to do nothing, he would take naked pictures of me put them up on this site, and when the men called to book my services I would have them come to a motel room where he would be waiting in the bathroom and rob them. I began to think all I have to do is take a few pictures. No one I knew would be on those sites, no one would see them. Slim said we could stay in the motel room. My Grandma had started to work my nerves. I was ready to get out of her house so I agreed. The first couple of times it worked like a charm we did it just like Slim had said. We were really on our Bonnie and Clyde flow until Slim switched it up. He said we had to figure something else out because it was costing too much to keep switching motels every time we hit a lick. Slim convinced me it wouldn't be that bad, he would be right in the other room. He said all I had to do was lay there the guys would do all the work. "We can make $200 in 20 minutes," he bragged. "This is not what I signed up for", I argued. Slim became so upset he slapped me and said: "all the shit I have done for your ungrateful ass you can't do this one thing." I showed him how much I appreciated him every chance I got. I wasn't ungrateful, I just didn't want to be with no other man but Slim. I couldn't believe that he was even asking me to do this. In the end, I did it. What choice did I have? Go back to my grandma's house so she could say "I told you his ass wasn't shit." Within a month I was getting so many hits on my page, men were running through me like a drive-up window. Slim could not stop talking about how much money we were making. We? How many dicks had Slim sucked? Did he need KY just to tolerate the pain? Did he get sick to his stomach every time his cell phone chirped or even worse, a knock on the door? It's funny how fast our equal partnership became a dictatorship. I worked when he said work. I ate when he said to eat. I even spoke, dressed and acted the way he said, yet I never saw a dime of the money. Slim kept all the money and anything I needed I had to get it from him. I even had to ask him for sanitary products when it was that time of the month. Damn, how did I get here? Even the money I was making wasn't enough for Slim, he started hitting his own licks and of course, he kept all the money. I can't lie, I was relieved when I got the collect call from the County. Slim had got caught sticking someone up and was in jail. After a few weeks, the relief turned into terror, anxiety, and fear. How was I going to pay for this room where would I find money to eat? It then occurred to me that I didn't need Slim. I knew the game, I could hold us down. Shortly us became me and I couldn't believe how much money I was making. When I thought about it, I got pissed. What the hell did Slim do with all the money I had made? I became my own boss and I worked it just like Slim, actually I worked it better than Slim. I never knew I could be so seductive, so manipulative, so raunchy. I did whatever I had to do to get that paper.

I despise the men that came through here, wanting all kind of nasty shit done to them. Watching them put their wedding ring back on as they exited my room. The smell that I can't wash away. The feeling I get in the pit of my stomach when I think of how many of them it has been. The fear I feel every time I shut my door after a trick arrives. The shame that overtakes me each time I look in the mirror. But hey, this is all I know!

"Whose Little Girl Am I? Anyone Who Has Money to Buy." -Nina Simone, 1966

Dr. Kisha Roberts Tabb

26 SOMETHING NEW

> "They say you can't turn a bad girl good. But once a good
> girl's gone bad, she's gone forever..."

-Jay Z, 2002

I was so used to dating ballers and dope dealers that a conversation on a college campus about the ability of God and how he responds to confessions was a welcome experience. I had never dated a man that I could have a conversation about God and religion with, without it becoming instructional or me doing all the talking and them pretending to care. These conversations became frequent some about religion, my experience as a single mother, work, and forgiveness.

This was really something new, and I liked it. He seemed to be so into me, always intrigued by the wealth of knowledge I possessed, at least at first. He also seemed to be really into my daughter, always including her in our plans, which was a good thing because Ebony had graduated so I didn't have a babysitter anymore. We spent a lot of time at my apartment; I didn't like having my baby out late at night. I would cook and we would watch Disney movies and shows until it was time to put my baby to bed. When my car went out he gave me his to get back and forth to work.

It seemed like an act of God when my close friend moved out of my apartment and into one across the hall from him. Now the people that I spent the most time with lived in the same place. When I would sleep over his house I could leave my daughter across the hall. He had roommates and I was never comfortable with my daughter being around too many men. To be honest I was hesitant for her to see me with even this man in that way. She had never been around another man besides her father. With the exception of dinner and a movie, I was sure not to act like this was a real relationship in front of her. This wasn't that hard because my good girlfriend was also around a lot so we all seemed like really close friends. I hadn't consciously recognized how close the three of us really were. So close that when my good girlfriend would cook she would always take a plate next door to him. They discussed going to the movies on weekends that I was going home and she would even drop him off to my apartment so he wouldn't lose his parking space.

My something new had blossomed really fast and before long I couldn't hide it from my baby or anyone else. I was in a full blown relationship with this mighty man of God. Like everything else that was important, I began to pray about it. I asked God if this man did not have both my daughter's and my best interest at heart to send me a sign. Funny thing about signs, if you are not careful your desire will overshadow your discernment. Seeing no sign I decided to take this relationship to an intimate level. Shortly after I realized that I was getting bacterial infections quite frequently, in a conversation with my good girlfriend I learned that she got them quite often as well.

He was younger than me and I was graduating that year so we begin to discuss how we would maintain a relationship with me going to study abroad after graduation and him returning back to school after the summer. We devised a plan for my time out of the county. I opened a yahoo account so we could email each day. I emailed and kept a journal so that we could discuss my experience upon my return. However, the return emails got less frequent, often weeks passing without hearing from him, and when I did the emails were quick and to the point. The time had come for me to return to the states. Our first night together he caught me up with what was going on with everyone including my good girlfriend who had also graduated with me the previous semester. He was well versed in her current state of affairs, and that didn't sit well with me. I questioned how he knew so much about her. He told me that he had talked to her once over the summer. I thought to myself; that must have been a long conversation because he knew a lot about her. I decided to run this by a mutual friend who informed me that my suspicions were valid and also revealed that my something new was nothing new at all. He was like every other guy just a little slicker and much grimier than any of the others. It turns out that we all were really close. To my surprise, we were all in an intimate relationship. I learned that the patience that he had displayed while I contemplated becoming intimate with him was helped by my good girlfriend. She had already become sexually involved with him and they continued to sleep together throughout our entire relationship.

"I feel so lost don't know why this has happened to me, um my closest friend...but my man you laid and I'm betrayed..." -Kelly Price, 1998

Betrayed twice- she knew everything there was to know about me and he pretended to love me. How do you recover from this? Enough was enough or was it?

27 THOUGHT HE WAS DIFFERENT

I had just closed and moved into my new home. This was supposed to be a happy time but this man just will not go away. How can someone do as much as he has done and then protest you breaking up with him? Phone call after phone call, argument after argument, I was so over this. Then the phone at my desk rang. I answered ready to argue when an unfamiliar male voice said; "Hey I know this seems strange but I could tell something was wrong yesterday during our meeting." Shocked and still somewhat annoyed I remained silent. "I could be wrong but you looked like you had been crying and in my experience when a woman looks like she's been crying it usually has something to do with a man." All I could do was laugh, he had hit it on the head. "I just wanted to call you and tell you that you are worth so much more and if he cannot see that then he don't deserve your tears. You have so much going for yourself, don't sell yourself short." Immediately the tears began to silently flow, the last thing he said before hanging up was "any man should be grateful to have a woman like you, I hope today is better than yesterday" and just like that, he had hung up. I sat there crying because the truth was it wasn't any better. It was the same ole thing day after day.

From that day forward we developed an amazing friendship. We discussed basketball, the kids on our caseloads, and our own children. We ate lunch together, attended cultural events, and bounced ideas off one another. Eventually, our friendship had manifested into something more.

I thought this was my forever. The way he looked at me. The way my body heated up from his mere touch. The anxiousness I felt when I heard his car approaching. The song "*When We Made Love*", doesn't come close to describing our intimate experiences. I still remember our first kiss it was as if I had been waiting on a kiss like that my entire life. I can still hear him tell me he loved me for the first time, the nervousness in his voice, the hesitance that accompanied each word, "I... love ... you," along with the sigh of relief when I replied I love you more.

My grandmother would always say "never love a man more than he loves you, and if you do, don't ever let him know."

Had I broken the golden rule, had I set the entire tone of our relationship? Did I love him more? In the beginning, I didn't think so. He called me every morning; we met for lunch as much as possible. We walked downtown hand in hand. He always spoke to me so softly, always so attentive. He acted as my protector, my fixer, and my number one fan. We would spend hours on end on the phone. Nothing was off limits. To say we fell in love would be a lie. We learned to love each other on purpose. I had never experienced anything like this; he had to be my forever.

"You got me trippin' got me looking in the mirror different thinking I'm flawed because you inconsistent..." -Cardi B. 2018

The time between an unanswered phone call and return call grew longer and longer. When called to his attention, the unanswered phone calls were returned immediately but from quiet secluded places. He began to hang out with a new group of friends, none of whom I knew. Attending gatherings that I was never invited to. The bathroom conversation between his cousin and myself, regarding my surprise party I hadn't had. You know, the wrong girl conversation. A cell phone that hadn't rung in years, only vibrated, and a keyed car.

Just when I had convinced myself that none of this meant anything, I received a late night phone call. You don't know me but, at first, I thought someone was playing a joke on me. I'm way too old for this. Is this for real? Is this what my forever will look like? Of course he didn't know her and of course, I went along with it; he was my forever. Actually, I didn't go along, I got lost. I got competitive. I went all in. I became everything that he required, attempting to eliminate the need for another woman. Guess what, it didn't work. Not only could I not be everything he needed, there were things that he desired that I didn't possess. Even knowing this, I kept on fighting, right up until she arrived at my house. See I wasn't the only one competing, so was she. Just like I had been on a mission to eliminate her position, her goal was for me to know she had solidified hers. I could no longer ignore the late night text messages, the hang-ups, the silent ringtones, the unanswered phone calls, and the disappearing acts. Here was the proof I needed. In my mind, she had just blown up my entire world. The truth was, there had been a bomb under my bed for years. She had just taken the pin out. As crazy as it sounds and as sick as her late night visit made me, I was so glad to know that I wasn't crazy. I appreciated the confirmation that my discernment was real. On the other hand, every piece of confidence that I possessed drove away with her. How did she know where I lived? Why didn't he protect me? Why had he protected her? What did she have that I didn't? The thought of him kissing her for the first time, telling her that he loved her and giving her a pet name drove me insane. Did he touch her like he touched me, did he make lifelong plans with her? Did she know his kids and did he bring her around his family? The hurt turned into anger and the anger turned into embarrassment. I questioned myself and my own value. The thought of life without him paralyzed me so much that it took me three days to get out of bed. But on the third night, I did. I stared at myself until I began to see the woman that I was before I met him. I saw a whole woman. The pieces I had allowed myself to be broken into slowly molded back together. I saw the daughter of a king. I looked until I found ME again.

Dr. Kisha Roberts Tabb

28 It's Not You It's Me

"Take self-inventory, you're woman and you're glory. Leave the bad things behind..."

-Aretha Franklin, 1976

As women, we often times look to ourselves when men cheat, reject, and abandon us. We own all of their mess. We try to figure out what it is that the other woman has that we don't. We stalk her social media page, examine her clothes, her weaves, her shoes. We often find that she's not cuter, she dresses alright, a little cheap for our liking, but cute stuff. We discover that there is nothing special about her, she could have been anyone. So if it's not her then it must be you. If you are like me, you try and figure out what's wrong with you. I'm telling you I have been there a million times. Changing my hair going on a diet, living at the gym, buying a new brand of make-up, just to get his attention and lose it again.

It's ironic that the very things that attract a man to you become the very thing that he despises in the end. I can't tell you how many guys have told me how smart I am. "You not like the other women I dated." "You so confident." "Girl you got it going on!" It's amazing how quickly this turns into "You think you know everything."   "You too smart for your own good." "I have never dealt with this from a woman." "Who you think you are?" All those things he loved so much about you in the beginning, become turn-offs when you use those same characteristics. According to him, you deserve the world until you ask for it, then you ain't never satisfied. We find ourselves purposefully shrinking. Trying to make ourselves small enough to accommodate his sense of manhood.

Women are born with a certain amount of intuition. Grandma said, "it's God's reward for having to endure childbirth." We always know. We can lie and say we had no idea but deep down, we always know. As women, we find ourselves stuck between knowing and saying. If we tell them how much we know, they will work harder to hide. If we pretend not to know, we become enraged and bitter. If we confront their insecurities, we're accused of beating a Black man down. In the words of Cardi B, "we find ourselves stuck between the mud and the dirt." The truth is no matter how hard you try, you can only be you. Trying to be who others want you to be is way too exhausting. Eventually, the mask comes off and if you can't recognize yourself in the mirror there is a problem.

We have to decide how much we are willing to accept. We have to remind ourselves that it's ok to be ourselves and to be by ourselves. Most times, we come into a relationship still healing from the last one, telling our new man everything that we accepted from the last one. In essence, we tell men how much they can get away with. We give other people the key to our happiness. I have decided to keep the key to my own happiness. My granny also said, "God will take you through the same thing over and over until you learn the lesson that was intended." I decided that I had learned my lesson. I was done. I was going to make sure that I entered into the next relationship whole, lacking nothing. I would be looking above for validation and honoring everything that I had experienced. Taking the lessons learned, and leaving whatever I didn't need behind. All limits were off; I am now walking in my worth. I realized that it's never been about them, it's always been ME.

29 40 Days to Clarity

By Briana Roberts

Months away from turning 30, yet I hate my life and everything about it. I want a do-over, God. Not a die and come back again do-over. A do-over where the place I call home and share with my boyfriend is no longer a revolving door for him to use for the girls he meets on dating apps. A do-over where I actually make a living doing something that I am passionate about, something fulfilling. A do-over where I don't eat my insecurities stress and pain to cope with the fact that I am committed to someone who cheats more than he breathes. This can't be what You had in store for me! Do I not matter to you either? God, I want Your very best and I am willing to lose everything to get it. What did

You have in your will for me when You created me because this can't be it?

God speaks, " I'm going to bring you full circle. Everything I've always intended for you I've shown you, but you talked yourself out of it again and again. So here goes, your husband I have for you, you've known over 10 years. Remember when you prayed and asked me for certain qualities in a husband and I told you he was it with everyone and gave you proof? You ran away. You said he deserved someone better, more accomplished, with a degree and a good heart. Next, I told you that you were a teacher and a leader. I told you that you would be a millionaire and you would mentor and teach people in your industry. Yet you were worried about not knowing how to do nail designs and stopped doing nails all together to put your all into a job that was barely paying $35,000 a year. So, I am going to bring these promises back to you but you have to get ready and you have to trust the process. So make a choice, Do you want to keep living your will or do you now want to really live Mine?"

Can I finally do this and do it God's way? The man God has for me to marry, God is right, he's already proven to be everything I asked God for in a man. I've been asking God for those characteristics for years in a man. At least the last 7 years. But am I worth him? God has told me since I was a teenager I would be a multi-millionaire, but I can't really be trusted with that money. Why would I deserve all that money? Plus money is the root of all evil. I've seen it change people. I've seen it.

God interjects, "BRI! If I tell you the best I have in store for you why do you still keep talking yourself out of it? If I tell you you're worth it, where are you getting the impression that you're not? Before you make your decision, you need to figure out why you are trying to convince yourself that you are not worth My Love, My Blessings or to simply receive the desires 'I' have placed in you? You keep pushing those desires away! You have to get to the bottom of why?"

He's right! Usually, it's a person's upbringing so let me start there. Let's see. BigDaddy (my grandfather) loved me in a way that I really don't know if I will ever find in any other human. Even though he was my grandfather, he showed me a Daddy's love. Took me to and from school most of my life. He talked to me about the importance of making an honest living and taking care of myself. According to him, I just had to finish high school and from there figure out how I am going to maintain a living. Even as an adult he calls me every evening to make sure I made it in the house ok. Calls randomly to make sure I have food in my fridge or gas in my car. Some will say he spoils me but I call it Love!!

Then there's my Auntie Sharon! Another one who would pick me up from school, take me shopping for clothes and simply cared for me. Almost any time she left the house she took me with her. When we were home she taught me how to play card games like Solitaire and Uno and games on the computer. I would always fall asleep in her room watching movies. She taught me how I treat others is a good reflection of how I treat and respect myself. If I ever want to know how I see myself, look at what I say to and about others and how I treat them because that all comes from somewhere within me.

Lastly, there was my Grandmother! She would come into my room at night and check to make sure I was breathing or simply pray over me. She was always so giving to others and not just anything but from her heart. Family and God were everything to her and she made sure she taught me the same. She told me one day, "If you never go to church or become active in a church, even if you don't understand the Bible, just never forget to pray. Make sure you talk to God every day, especially when you wake up."....So, I had a loving upbringing!

God says, "You haven't mentioned your parents. What about them?"

What about them God?

"How did they show love to you?"

I don't know/ They're my parents and I love them. I honestly don't know what to say about how they loved me. I'm sure they do but I don't know how. Ok, God, if they love me then why did my mother let her husband curse me clean out when I was 13 simply because I misunderstood what he wanted me to do at the time? Since then, she let him kick me out at 18 because I forgot to wash the dishes and let him bully me around the house until I left. She left me alone with him as a teenager just so he can tell me things like, "You act like you're stupid. I don't understand why your family cares so much about you because you're nothing like your sister. She is actually pretty, smart and independent. They have reasons to be crazy about her." Mind you, my sister, who is 9 years older than me, already graduated from college and very much an adult at this time. He even shared with me that he doesn't like that my mother loves me as much as she does and that it is different from the way she loves him. Even 'til this day he doesn't speak to me and has my number blocked. Why does he hate me so much? More importantly, why is she ok with him hating me so much? Aren't they supposed to be equally yoked? Honestly, God, I'm tired.

You asked about both parents. As for my Father, God I really don't know. I see a lot of similarities between him and me. I remember living with my Father for a school year after my grades went down to C's, D's and F's. They came up when I lived with him though, but I was scared of the consequences of having bad grades in his house. What those consequences were exactly, I don't know but I knew he did NOT play! I mean look at who he raised. My oldest sister has her Ph.D. and finished every degree she has while raising my niece. She did all of that and more based on her endurance and everything he taught her. My second oldest sister is an Anesthesiologist! Making more money than I ever believed I could make. Then there's my 3rd oldest sister who isn't his biological daughter but who he took in as his own. She went to U of I Urbana and got her bachelors and always had pretty good jobs making pretty good money. My brother mutated cells his last year of high school for a science fair project. He won the school and State Science Fair. The purpose was to uncover the cause and possible cures of Alzheimer's disease. He's so well rounded that he couldn't decide if he wanted to be a politician, attorney or doctor. Meanwhile, he's currently traveling from London to Africa establishing workshops to help reform prisoners to prepare them to go back into society. Then my two younger sisters each have a bachelor's degree. One achieved her degree despite having cerebral palsy and the other is just about finished with her master's degree in bio-engineering. Then there's me! I couldn't finish my associates, let alone a bachelor's degree. I enjoy the beauty industry and finished cosmetology school but that's really it. I've had 10 jobs from the time I was 18 to now going on 30. I've been fired from 2 jobs. Yet, I still don't see a point in going back to school unless I do it just to prove people wrong who don't think I can finish or don't expect me to. God, why wasn't he more hands-on with raising me? Even in my adult years, he's talked about establishing a relationship but really, we haven't. We go months without speaking. I can't help but wonder if he showed as much interest in me as he did in the rest of his children, blood and adopted, would I be further in life? God, why didn't he make me more of a priority? Simply pick me up for dinner from time to time when I was younger? Take me to various things that parents do with their children to spend time with them? Actually get to know me! I don't see him as a bad person. I think he's hilarious and like I said, I see a lot of similarities in our ways but at the end of the day we don't know each other as well as we should.

So, what is the lesson in this God? So what they weren't ideal. I still love both of my parents and will honor them as such. I still don't understand what this all means.

God speaks, "Do you feel like you matter to your parents?"

Honestly God, for the younger me I would say No, barely at all. For the older me, I see it as they do what is convenient for them. I don't believe they've intentionally tried to hurt me in the process but ultimately they do what is most convenient for them and I get the scraps. But again, now what?

God, "Now you know why you lack self-worth. The two people that were chosen to show you that you were worthy of the blessings I have in store for you and the purpose I put on your life stood in the back of the line and allowed others to do what they were supposed to do. This doesn't mean that you resent them in any way because keep in mind I knew what they were going to do with you, that is why I made sure you consistently had people that would supply you with the Love and Wisdom you needed to get you to where you are now. This simply means that now you are clear that a hole is there and where it originated, now it is your own self-love that has to start filling that hole before we enter this next chapter of life and before you can receive the blessings and miracles I have for you. Get ready, because I'm about to bring back everything the devil tried to take from you!"

40 Days of fasting; only consuming water, praying a minimum of 3 times a day while reading the word in the morning at night and sometimes during the day I finally gained clarity. I learned that not only was I capable of fully loving myself but that I was worthy of God's love. God's been waiting to give me His very best in every way I could imagine. No more do I worry about if God is going to deliver everything he promised me. No more do I question worth. No more do I question if I am enough in this life in

general. I am a breathing testimony that is fearfully and wonderfully made. I am loved by a God that wants to do exceedingly, abundantly and above all that I can think of ask for or imagine. I've definitely had more than a taste and see experience. Trusting God while learning the Love of God and how to apply it to me brought me to and through the fast. Greater is He that is in me than he that is in the world. In You God, I will forever be able to stand. I never want to let You down. I Love you Holy One!

Dr. Kisha Roberts Tabb

30 AND SO IT BEGINS

> "When I thought it was nothing left I do believe I found myself..."
>
> -*Aretha Franklin, 1976*

We talked on the phone almost every day, probably more than we did when we lived under the same roof. I was so proud of my sissy, she was living her dream of going to medical school. I had finished up my Master's degree about two years ago and was feeling a little stuck as to what was next. On one of our early morning calls my Sissy asked me, "why don't you get a doctorate, like a Ph.D.?"

I was so sick of school, the thought of writing more papers scared me. I had thought about going and getting a massage license but it seemed like that was working backward, so I scrapped that idea. "I don't like school like that."

I still can't believe I had finished my Masters in Public Administration.

Now she was finishing up her first year of medical school and was doing very well. My sister was in medical school; I bragged different. I told any and everyone who would listen that my sister was going to be a doctor. One doctor in the family was good enough for me. But she wouldn't let up. "You should at least apply, you know how dope it would be for Daddy to say both my daughters are doctors."

Now, that got my attention. Whenever you put my daddy in the mix it changed the whole motivation. When she first said something about me going back to school, it all seemed so unattainable. She was supposed to be the doctor I was born to be a probation officer. But she was right Dr. Kim & Dr. Kisha Roberts did have a ring to it.

She and Daddy had often mentioned law school since I love to argue but a Ph.D. seemed a bit farfetched. My sister had always been the smart one I can't believe that she thought that I could actually do this. By the time I arrived at my job I was ready to research and apply for schools. I applied to Olivet Nazarene University and my lil sister Briana took off work and rode with me to the interview. She had the best gospel playlist and she made sure that my spirit was right when I arrived. Before entering the room I called MaDear for a prayer. Walking in the room I felt like I could take over the world, walking out I felt like the world was out of my reach. Like I had expected I received a letter, "Thank you for your interest in our program..." I didn't have to continue reading to know that this was a rejection letter. Ok; I had kept my word and applied, but it didn't look like I was going to be able to be the 2nd Dr. Roberts.

I attempted to avoid the conversation with my sissy but she asked, "What's going on with your applications?"

I said, "I didn't get in."

"That is only one school where else did you apply?"

"A few more," I responded, knowing I was lying.

That morning when I got to work I began looking at other schools. I liked the sound of community psychology so I decided to try my luck. I looked up the requirements and again doubt crept up, they required a GRE. I've never been a good test taker but was too embarrassed to call and tell her that I was afraid to take the GRE. I purchased some study books, borrowed one from Dr. Lewis, started studying, and signed up for the test. Beginning my application before I took the test, the last thing I needed to submit was my test scores. I didn't do that great but I submitted them anyway. I was so surprised when I received the call for my interview with National Louis University. I had been here before so I was not getting my hopes up high. I didn't tell anyone about the interview except for my sisters, my daughter, and Chuck. Although I felt better about this program I still would not get my hopes up high in fact, I didn't ever follow up.

July 2011, I was sitting in the Atlanta airport and I began to look through my emails as we waited to board our flight. There it was, an email from NLU; I guess I didn't get in. I opened the email and the first thing I saw was "CONGRATULATIONS," I didn't read any further I just began to shake. "OH MY GOD," I had gotten in! After telling my co-workers, who thought that I was going crazy, I called my Sissy, "Dr. Roberts, I got in, I'm going to get my Ph.D."

Dr. Kisha Roberts Tabb

31 DISCOVERING PASSION

I have always had a passion for girls. For as long as I can remember I was teaching them dances for the annual fashion show. I would go back to my junior high every day to teach the girls on the cheerleading team cheers and formations. So I thought that teaching was my passion. I tried my hand as an education major for a minute while in college, but like most things that seemed hard, I quit. After returning from Ghana I got a job as a seventh-grade teacher at a parochial school, the pay was horrible but I loved the connection I made with the kids, especially the girls. We would meet after school to discuss issues they were having. As a teacher, I would make my students write journal entries upon arriving to class and on Friday I would take them home and respond to the entries. Before long the journals became advice columns for my girls. They would write down a problem and I would respond. The day I told them I was leaving to take a job as a probation officer all of the girls cried, including one that would use her journal entries to tell me how much she disliked me and how I thought I was cute. I struggled with leaving my babies and wept right along with my students. Had I just agreed to walk away from my passion?

I hit the hallways of Juvenile Court running. I was a hands-on person and although undiagnosed, I am pretty sure I have ADHD. I became bored very easily, so shortly after arriving, I wrote a program, for girls of course. Project Dance was a social, emotional learning program for court-involved girls that utilized dance as a tool to express themselves. I remember when the flyer first went out and it was called Dance Therapy, a group of women who worked as art therapist protested the program saying I was not a dance therapist so it was unethical. For this reason, it became "Project Dance". Personally, I think it was a much cooler name anyway. We began each class with a topic, that topic was tied to the song and movement. We danced and ended with an activity that would allow us to unpack the emotion that may have been evoked by the music and movement. I loved doing this program. We went from operating in the main courthouse to expanding to the south suburban courthouse. Meeting twice a week, I spent four days of the week facilitating the program. I began to think that dance must be my passion, after all, I was able to use it in such a creative way. I always left groups so fulfilled and validated. Yes, this must be my passion. I began to think that there must be more I can do with this passion I had for dance. So I researched master's programs. I found a program that seemed perfect, it was a dance therapy graduate program at Columbia University. I was so excited, then I read the requirements and, like so many times before, the fear that I would not be able to do it paralyzed me and I decided to look for another passion. I was able to get my fix for dance in my church's dance ministry even taught some African dance classes at a few places.

Years later I became a California Girls Circle Keeper and again I thought I am really good at facilitating these groups, this must be my passion. I was great at girls circle, although many around me made comments that someone from the clinical department should be facilitating the groups. After two years of circle keeping, I decided that girls should not have to come through the system to experience the lessons from women with similar experiences that looked like them. I called four of the most dynamic women I could think of Natia, Tamar, Jene, and Sherri. After one meeting over breakfast, SOCIAL Butterfly Foundation was born. We took off like a rocket, our foundation was being recognized by judges, police officers, pastors, and we were doing some really cool things with our girls. Finally, I must have found my passion SOCIAL Butterfly was it. Our first year we had raised $13,000 for our girls. We used the money to give them an amazing Presentation Ball.

SOCIAL Butterfly was an amazing experience, but I still wasn't sure it was that thing that I was looking for. Due to my success in fundraising for SOCIAL Butterfly, I was approached by a former co-worker to assist with fundraising in her new position, the director of The Chicago Dream Center. After hearing about the work they were doing with women I decided to donate all of the money as long as she agreed to dedicate the space to my mother.

After donating the money I began to receive emails and texts messages from the women on the farm enjoying the items that they were able to purchase with my donation. Items included a barbecue grill, a picnic table, and other outdoor items. The pictures were followed by invitations to visit the farm. To be honest, I did not want to engage, I just wanted to give some money and feel good about it. I didn't want to go because it was my understanding that this farm was for women who were recovering from addiction. Immediately, I became that little girl standing on the corner of 37th and King Drive, still angry at my mom for leaving so she could go get high. Each time, I declined, not wanting to project my negative energy on these women while they were attempting to overcome their addiction. Then, I received a call from my former co-worker asking me to go on a ride along with Rose of Sharon, a ministry under the Chicago Dream Center. I found out that this was an outreach ministry that targeted those affected by human trafficking. Intrigued, I agreed. I had no idea how much that YES would impact my life. I had agreed to do the first run, which met at seven. We prayed and hit the streets returning at eleven. After the first run, I decided to stay for the second run. This time we went all over from the north side to out west and then out south. While in the West Lawn area we drove past a lady who approached the van. All night we had approached the women but this woman was approaching us and she was quoting scripture. The team of three got out of the car, before long this woman was speaking in tongues, the team leader came back to the van and asked my former co-worker to come out for back-up. The lady that they were praying for began to speak in a demonic tone going back and forth from tongue to scripture. The prayer warriors were matching her with scripture and tongue. As I watched from the van I was paralyzed. I had never seen anything like this. I had never experienced a spiritual encounter so strong in my life. It was as though everything had ceased. There was no one on the street at the time, only the woman and us. The wind had picked up so much, the trees began to bend, yet I was not afraid. I could feel the presence of two spirits that of which was holy and that of something evil. Once the woman had been slain in the spirit and was laying on the ground, the wind slowed, the trees went back to their natural upright position, the cars and people on the streets picked right up where they left off. Completely unprepared for what I had just experienced I sat there unable to speak, so I watched. I watched these women embrace women working and walking the streets. I watched them pray with these women. I watched the light that these women had brought to such dark places. It was like I was lost in a trance just watching. My trance was broken when I saw the lights from the

Burger King sign at 47th and Damen. The van began to slow down and the next team got out of the van. I was startled when a woman darted out in front of the van in an attempt to evade the women offering prayer. She came to a sudden stop and turned around, I swear I saw my mother's face on this woman. She had her same build and all. You got four minutes, come on and pray, she said. The women surrounded her and began to pray. The prayer was so powerful that the man who had been accompanying the woman came in and asked, "Can you pray for me as well." I was watching true prayer warriors, in the street in the middle of the night praying for prostitutes and pimps. Now, this was passion. The next Friday and every Friday thereafter I was out there too. I had become one of these warriors and I loved it. This was it, this is what I had been chasing, and finally, I had discovered my passion. I was born to assist women, women who had been lost, women who had been turned out, women who

need grace, women like my mother.

32 BEAUTIFUL SURPRISE

"Whatever you came to teach me I am here to learn..."

-India Arie, 2002

Over the nine years that we had been together, we had been through so much. Sometimes I asked myself had I been a fool to stay. Although we had broken up a million times, in my heart I knew that there was no other man for me. The problem was I wasn't sure if he shared my truth.

"It's almost like I knew this man from another life, like maybe I was his husband and he was my wife..." -India Arie, 2002

For years, all I wanted was to be his wife. Yet I felt like I was being denied my title. I had been playing the part for years yet I was nothing more than a glorified girlfriend. I had begun to wrap my head around the fact that maybe being his wife was not in the cards for me. In the midst of this revelation, God began to put it in my spirit to pray for married couples. Like with everything else, I questioned God. Because He is all knowing, what had seemed like a request soon became an undeniable demand. I complied. Each time, it seemed so cruel - I was praying to strengthen in others the very thing that I wanted so bad for myself. God told me to pray for my ex and his wife. I began to pray for complete restoration. I prayed for the man I wanted to be my husband but God had made it clear that I was not to pray to be his wife—He had heard that prayer a million times. I was instructed to pray only for the man. So that's what I did. I prayed for his business ventures. I prayed for his confidence. I prayed for his relationship with God. I prayed that he would discover his purpose. I prayed that God would keep his kids safe. I prayed, I prayed and I prayed. Whenever I heard that whisper, I prayed. Whenever a person would randomly cross my mind, I knew that meant I was supposed to pray.

One Sunday while in praise and worship I received instruction to pray for peace for a woman that I had gone to school with. We were never close we knew each other and I knew that a year prior she had lost her son. So, I sat down and sent her a message via Facebook. Listening very carefully to what God wanted her to know, I told her that God said that she must stop blaming herself. God instructed me to tell her that it was not her fault, that she had been a good mother. This was so awkward. Most people thought I was pretty cool. I don't think anyone would expect me to become a prayer warrior. I was being stretched. Even the man that I was so in love with was looking at me funny. But I prayed without ceasing. I didn't know what God was doing but I knew that I had tried everything else. I was praying so much that I forgot about my desire to be **Mrs. Tabb.** I had become so happy just being Kisha. I had finally begun to like her, when I looked in the mirror I saw a dope chick staring back.

"I don't know the future hopes but I'm living in the moment..." -India Arie, 2002

While I was praying my man was looking, changing, growing. He began to talk about marriage, a life together. He asked about going to pre-marital classes, so we did. He dived in, participated, and developed his skills as a man. I began to see him through a new lens. But I was so accustomed to disappointment. Although it seemed like my prayers were being answered, I was still cautious. There had been talks of him popping the question but until he did I was going to continue to do me. While I was doing me, I had missed his efforts. On December 30th the day before my birthday while getting ready for work he said, "Let's go out to dinner tonight. Tomorrow is going to be crazy."

While I was getting dressed he said, "You've never worn that dress, you should wear it to dinner."

He was there to pick me up from work and we went to a sports bar. I know he didn't have me wear this dress to go to a sports bar. After a drink, he informed me that we needed to leave we had reservations. I couldn't believe that he had put so much effort into my birthday, I was so impressed.

"You are everything I ask for in my prayers...
You are a beautiful surprise..." -Indie Arie, 2002

We arrived at the restaurant and were escorted to our seat, cold based on where we were sitting near the window, I went to the washroom to warm up. Upon returning he had changed our table. We ordered, ate our food and then the waiter came over and asked if we would like to take a picture. I began to pose and he began to speak, still smiling looking at the camera, I tapped his arm he, was still speaking so I turned to look. He was still talking, joking, smiling and then he pulled the box out opened it and said

"Will you marry me?"

"I want you right here in my world here in my life, here in my soul I want the world to know…"

-Kem, 2010

As we left the restaurant, he asks me not to call anyone to tell them the news. He said he wanted my dad to be the first to know. So, we headed toward my Daddy's house. We opened the door, walked up the foyer stairs, and turned to see my entire family and all my friends. They were yelling, "Congratulations!" It was a full-blown engagement party. This was truly a beautiful surprise. I now could see that God had been preparing me through my instructional prayer. He allowed me to see the battle that was sure to come.

I wanted to go to city hall but he said that he needed to give me a wedding. He was concerned that every time I went to a wedding I would regret not having my own. This man gave me the most beautiful wedding anyone could imagine. With the sand under my feet, the waters of Lake Michigan in front, I walked toward the horizon and my man as the sun breathed color into the skylight upon the earth. Under the glorious dawn of a new day, I became **Mrs. Charles Tabb Jr.**

"Love him in every way that a woman can love a man from personal to universal but most of all it's unconditional..." India Arie, 2002

Dr. Kisha Roberts Tabb

33 THE POSSIBILITIES OF PASSION

"For I know the plans I have for you says the Lord."

-Jeremiah 29:11

God will take you to places and before people you never imagined.

Once while sitting in seven thirty service Pastor Hannah said, "God is about to bring your names up at tables that you've never been allowed to sit at among people you don't even know." I sat there thinking, "I wish." I had given so much to Juvenile Court over the years. I had created and implemented programs mentored young ladies and had been instrumental in bringing awareness around gender responsive issues including, domestic violence, the alarming rates of HIV and AIDs among African-Americans, and domestic human trafficking. I seemed to be running out of gas and, although

I loved what I did in Jumpstart, which was an educational program for minors on probation who had been displaced from both traditional and alternative educational settings, I did not feel impactful anymore. The only time I felt as if I was doing meaningful work these days was when I was out on Friday nights doing outreach.

One Friday night while in the van, we approached a group of what looked to be young girls. The closer we got, we noticed that they were transgender. As the driver continued pass the group, I asked to stop the van. "I would like to pray for them if they would let me." I got out of the car and walked towards the group of young people. I could tell that they were all minors. As I got closer I said, "Would you all like a rose and prayer tonight?" They began to walk off some even begin to run, all except for one. All of the others yelled, "Come on! Let's go!"

I heard a familiar voice say, "I can't, that's Ms. Roberts."

As we walked towards each other, I saw my student standing there in full drag.

"Hey, where have you been?" I asked. "I've missed you in class."

"I've missed you too Ms. Roberts," my student replied.

"Why didn't you run?" I asked, "Because I knew it was you and I just couldn't run from you."

I asked her, "how often have you worked in this area?"

Before she could answer, the entire crew was standing in front of me. I prayed for all of them and I embraced each one of them one by one and said, "God loves you." When I got to my student, I held on as long as I could because now that I knew her secret, I knew that she would not be in class Monday. This time I whispered, "God loves you and so do I."

As we parted, I saw a tear drop from her eye.

I winked and said, "Don't be ashamed, do better."

She smiled and I proceeded to the van. Not wanting to out my student, I went to the field PO and asked that she check on her.

I continued to work in Jumpstart while doing ministry on Friday night and I continued to see faces that I recognized from Juvenile Court. One young lady would even run away screaming, everyone on my team thought that she could see some kind of anointing on me. I knew it was because she knew I was a probation officer and she was on a juvenile arrest warrant. I was blown away by how many clients I was seeing out on the street on Friday nights. Working in Jumpstart and facilitating groups gave me an advantage, I knew almost every girl who came through the court. When I would see one of my co-workers' clients I would simply tell them to check on them. Occasionally I would tell co-workers what area to look for a client.

Before long the word had spread that I had the inside track on the whereabouts of clients on the run. I would get text messages with pictures of young ladies that said, "If you see her can you let me know?" I heard that a probation officer had become a human trafficking expert. I also heard that she was putting a conference together. It had been my plan to attend. Things don't always work as planned. I was asked to help out with the conference and so I did I invited every human trafficking person that I knew. I also presented a preventive workshop to the young ladies who attended. That presentation got the attention of the FBI Director of Crimes Against Children. A week later I was invited to the Cook County Human Trafficking Taskforce Meeting. During the meeting the question arose regarding areas where street-based prostitution was taking place and, like second nature, I started spitting off tracks, I even explained who was being sold on what tracks, teens, trans, and addicts. I received an invitation to join the taskforce after that meeting. From there everything happened so fast.

DCFS was having a conference and their Human Trafficking Advocate canceled, Lloyd's wife Tracey happened to be on the committee and was telling him about it. Tracey gave me my first opportunity to present at a professional conference. The confidence that I developed at that conference took me further than you could ever imagine. Next up, Juvenile Court Annual Symposium. Although I was asked to train at the symposium I was also asked if I could get one of the members of the FBI Human Trafficking Team to assist me in the training. At first, I felt offended, I got over it and contacted Crimes Against Children. The symposium was a two-day event the first day Dugan sent one of his agents and the second one he actually did it with me. I was facilitating a training with the

Director of Crimes Against Children of the Federal Bureau of Investigations. Unlike those who I had been working with for the last eleven years, he had major confidence in my ability and both he and his agent allowed me to do ninety percent of the training. Afterward, inviting me to assist in trainings that they were invited to do. Dugan was also in the midst of developing a human trafficking multi-disciplinary team and asked that I join the team. We would use the Denver Model. Modifying the assessment tool, using each of our experience to develop an assessment tool that would speak to our geographical area and the young people we encounter.

"You will look back and be so amazed..."
-Koryn Hawthorne, 2017

The entire time all this was going on I was finishing up my coursework for my doctorate program. I had reached the point of the program to complete our fieldwork. Since I had been working with an outreach team from the Dream Center, I reached out to the director to ask permission to complete my doctoral fieldwork under her, she agreed. Unfortunately, overwhelmed with her work and she forgot she said yes, never signing or logging hours. Two weeks before the final presentation was due, I reached out to my professor informing him that although I had been working outreach the field work never happened. We began to talk about the development of the MDT, the development of the assessment tool, as well as the trainings I had completed with the FBI. My professor suggested that I used that experience as my fieldwork project and like always Dugan came through in the clutch. I'm not bragging but my fieldwork presentation was so dynamic that the chair of my dissertation committee suggested that I change my dissertation topic from effects of gender-responsive programming on high-risk sexual behavior to human trafficking.

"So ain't no need for stressing and crying cause

he gon' show up just like he did the last time..."

-Koryn Hawthorne, 2017

Previously, my dissertation work had come to a complete halt. I was no longer interested and could not find the passion I had once had. After changing the topic, I emerged myself in the research continuing to train and speak on panels. Again, circumstances brought me another opportunity. My former co-worker and director of the Chicago Dream Center was asked to train the new hires at the Illinois Department of Juvenile Justice and was unable to she called me the day before and asked if I could. I did, doing so well that they invited me back four times, each time as a paid consultant. I continued to work alongside the FBI and other law enforcement agencies participating in Cross Country and the NBA Draft. I also continued to speak on panels and create awareness around domestic human trafficking.

When my pastor said that Sunday morning that "God is about to bring your name up," I thought he was talking about someone else. I never imagined that these were prophetic words for me. God has sat me before people that I would have never imagined including speaking before the Illinois Congressional Caucus which lead to the US Congressional Caucus where I spoke before several members of Congress including Nancy Pelosi who actually referred to my work during her keynote address. My passion has taken me so much further than my finances. My voice has been heard by many and I have impacted victims of trafficking in ways that I didn't even believe was possible.

"Ain't nobody stoppin' my shine, they try to break me try to take me out but I got Jesus on my side..." -Koryn Hawthorne, 2017

STUDY GUIDE

Life's journey is filled with ups and downs and a lot of curve balls. There are no right or wrong answers and the turns you take, good or bad, will allow you to grow. I do not have all of life's answers, but I do have some advice.

1.   Remain authentic. You are created based on His plan. Your walk, talk, and experiences will set you apart from everyone else. You do not need the validation of others, for you are qualified from above.

2.   Find the possibilities of your passion. Passion will take you much further than finances. The very thing you are willing to do for free with no acknowledgment will be your pathway to happiness, wealth, and purpose.

3.   Look for confirmation in the common places. It's that thing that keeps tugging on your

spirit, the quiet whisper, the promise made to you in your dreams. Those things will be confirmed in your everyday interactions. Often we look for a supernatural experience when your confirmation is sitting in your common places in plain sight.

4. Honor your journey. There is no such thing as just a coincidence. It is all part of the plan. You didn't just happen to be born, you were destined to be born. You are not just any woman, you are beautifully made in God's image. You are a world changer equipped with the very thing that someone else needs to make it to the next step in their own journey. You are not just enough, you are more than enough. You are pregnant with a gift that the world is waiting for you to birth. You are not powerless you are powerful. You are strength, you are love, compassion, and truth. You are a representation of greatness.

NOTES

Dr. Kisha Roberts Tabb

Whose Little Girl Am I?

Whose Little Girl Am I?

_____

_____

_____

_____

_____

_____

_____

_____

_____

_____

_____

Dr. Kisha Roberts Tabb

Whose Little Girl Am I?

Dr. Kisha Roberts Tabb

ABOUT THE AUTHOR

As the first Human Trafficking/ Gender Responsive/ LGBTQ Specialist for Cook County Juvenile Probation Department, Dr. Roberts - Tabb has worked alongside Stop IT, Sky Way Railroad, Center on Halsted, Not Your Shame, Children's Advocacy Center, Chicago Police Department, Cook County Sheriff's Office, Juvenile Temporary Detention Center, Department of Children and Family Services, and the FBI (specifically Operation Cross County 2015 , 2016, and 2017) to assure that the youth we service are afforded the best care and treatment possible without violating their dignity and safety while acting as a mentor and, often a mother figure.

Dr. Roberts-Tabb's gender-responsive work includes an independent study abroad at the University of Ghana Legon, Ghana, West Africa, looking women's contribution to the Ghanaian economy. Along with her work as a Cook County Juvenile Probation Officer, and years of academic research, Dr. Roberts-Tabb has become the expert on gender issues. Research and findings from her, MPA, Master's Capstone "The Effects of Gender Responsive Programming on Female Adolescent Recidivism" along with her professional and academic experiences lead to the development of "Project Dance" a gender-specific program that utilized cultural expression to combat issues that lead to the recidivism of female juvenile probation clients, along with the Social Butterfly Foundation, a rites of passage and mentoring program. Dr. Roberts-Tabb holds a B.A. in Politics and Government from Illinois State University, an M.P.A. from Governor State University, and a Ph.D. in the discipline of Community Psychology from National Louis University, Dissertation: Public Perceptions and Attitudes Regarding Domestic Sex Trafficking Victims. Research for her thesis,

The Effect of Gender-Specific Programming on the High-Risk Sexual Behavior of African-American Adolescent Girls and outreach and rescue ministry efforts led her to the area of urban human trafficking. Dr. Roberts-Tabb has worked with the Chicago Coalition on Urban Girls, Dream Center's Rose of Sharon Outreach Team, Not Your Shame, Cook County Human Trafficking Taskforce, CCHT Taskforce Training Subcommittee, Cook County Multi-Disciplinary Team, and Promise Taskforce to combat the trafficking of urban youth one person at a time.

The knowledge and passion that Dr. Roberts-Tabb possesses has impacted service providers nationally, recently sitting before the Congressional Caucus for Black Women and Girls in Washington D.C., along with the Illinois Congressional Caucus for Black Women and Girls. Training designed by Dr. Roberts-Tabb, "Identifying Trafficking Victims "have been implemented for Cook County Juvenile

Probation Officers, Illinois Juvenile Justice After Care Specialist, and Juvenile Temporary Detention Staff and Caseworkers. Dr. Roberts-Tabb has also conducted training for DCFS, Reclaim 13 First Responders, National Guard, Chicago Dream Center, and several high schools and colleges throughout the Chicagoland area around the topic of identifying urban trafficking victims. Dr. Roberts-Tabb has worked on the Human Trafficking Housing Pilot with the Administration for Children and Families in partnership with Housing and Urban Development which will assist trafficking survivors with the Housing Choice Vouchers. Dr. Roberts-Tabb has contributed to the book Grace, the Human Trafficking Law Enforcement Subcommittee Report, May 2018 and is currently working on the Chicago Report on the Conditions of Urban Girls.

Whose Little Girl Am I?

Made in the USA
Columbia, SC
14 April 2019